UNSTOPPABLE AFFIRMATIONS

UNSTOPPABLE AFFIRMATIONS

31 DAYS OF WORDS THAT TRANSFORM YOUR MIND AND LEVEL UP YOUR LIFE

LOU JONES

Unstoppable Affirmations: 31 Days of Words that Transform Your Mind and Level Up Your Life
Copyright © 2024 by Lou Jones

Published in Dallas, Texas, by Let's Go! Press

All rights reserved. No part of this publication may be reproduced, stored in a retrieval system, or transmitted in any form or by any means—electronic, mechanical, photocopy, recording, or any other—except for brief quotations in critical reviews or articles, without the prior permission of the publisher.

Unless otherwise stated, all Scripture quotations are taken from the Holy Bible, New International Version®, NIV®. Copyright © 1973, 1978, 1984, 2011 by Biblica, Inc.® Used by permission. All rights reserved worldwide.

Scripture quotations marked (KJV) are taken from King James Version (KJV): King James Version, public domain.

Scripture quotations marked NLT are taken from the New Living Translation, copyright © 1996, 2004, 2015 by Tyndale House Foundation. Used by permission of Tyndale House Publishers, Inc., Carol Stream, Illinois 60188. All rights reserved.

ISBN 978-1-7364439-2-7 (paperback)
ISBN 978-1-7364439-3-4 (hardcover)

Library of Congress Control Number: 2023924184

Printed in The United States
10 9 8 7 6 5 4 3 2 1

For my wife, Ruth, who has inspired and
helped me become a better version of myself,
and for my son Aiden, my unstoppable why.
I love you both to the moon and back.

CONTENTS

Foreword..**ix**
Introduction: Level Up Your Life..**xiii**

Affirmations to Level Up Your Spirit and Soul
Day 1: Affirmations to Grow Spiritually...............................**3**
Day 2: Affirmations to Increase Self-Love............................**7**
Day 3: Affirmations to Increase Self-Esteem and Self-Worth....**11**
Day 4: Affirmations to Overcome Negative Thoughts.............**15**
Day 5: Affirmations to Let Go of Stress, Worry, and Anxiety...**19**

Affirmations to Level Up Your Health and Wellness
Day 6: Affirmations for Health, Healing, and Wellness..........**25**
Day 7: Affirmations for Better Self-Care............................**29**
Day 8: Affirmations for Better Mental Health.....................**33**
Day 9: Affirmations for Overcoming Depression..................**37**
Day 10: Affirmations for Improving Your Body Image...........**41**
Day 11: Affirmations for Weight Loss................................**45**

Affirmations to Level Up Your Success and Abundance
Day 12: Affirmations for Landing a New Job......................**53**
Day 13: Affirmations for Success at Work...........................**57**
Day 14: Affirmations for Promotion..................................**63**
Day 15: Affirmations for Abundance and Prosperity.............**65**
Day 16: Affirmations for Entrepreneurial Success.................**71**

CONTENTS

Affirmations to Level Up Your Attitude and Confidence
Day 17: Affirmations to Believe in Yourself..........................**79**
Day 18: Affirmations to Increase Confidence........................**85**
Day 19: Affirmations to Overcome Fear..............................**89**
Day 20: Affirmations to Become More Grateful and Thankful...**93**
Day 21: Affirmations to Take Personal Responsibility.............**97**

Affirmations to Level Up Your Relationships and Family
Day 22: Affirmations for Improving Your Relationship..........**103**
Day 23: Affirmations for Finding Love, Romance, and a
        Healthy Relationship..**107**
Day 24: Affirmations for a Great Marriage..........................**111**
Day 25: Affirmations for Positive Parenting........................**117**
Day 26: Affirmations for Healing a Broken Heart.................**123**
Day 27: Affirmations for Letting Go and Moving Forward....**127**

Affirmations to Level Up Your Productivity
Day 28: Affirmations to Develop a Success Mindset.............**133**
Day 29: Affirmations to Help You Achieve Your Goals..........**137**
Day 30: Affirmations to Stay Focused................................**139**
Day 31: Affirmations to Overcome Procrastination..............**143**

About the Author..**147**
Acknowledgements...**149**
References...**151**

FOREWARD

It brings me immense joy and pride to introduce you to the transformative world of *Unstoppable Affirmations: 31 Days of Words that Transform Your Mind and Level Up Your Life*. I am not only honored to be connected to the brilliant mind behind this book but have also been profoundly impacted by the principles and affirmations presented within its pages.

Let me take you back to the roots of this book, to the man behind the affirmations, my husband. Our journey together has been one marked by shared dreams, mutual support, and a commitment to growth. Affirmations are not mere words on paper for us. They are one of the threads that weave the fabric of our shared successes and individual achievements. Personally, I have used affirmations as one of the tools to help me realize my goals, from financial milestones to navigating uncertain career transitions. I can remember, like it was yesterday, the early days of my career and speaking aloud daily an affirmation I had written. The affirmation stated I would be making six figures within the next seven years, and I achieved it in five years. Within the twists and turns of life, affirmations became my allies, helping me rewire limiting beliefs and fuel my desire to turn aspirations into reality.

When I was single and seeking a godly spouse, I daily encouraged myself to stay focused and wait for God's best with an affirmation similar to the "Affirmations for Finding Love, Romance, and a Healthy Relationship" within this very book. Today, I am happily married to the man of my affirmations and my dreams!

As the wife of the author, I've witnessed firsthand and up close the tool of affirmations work in his life and the lives of those he's coached. He is not just qualified, but uniquely positioned, to guide you through this journey of transformation. As a certified life coach and ordained pastor, he brings both expertise and a genuine passion for elevating minds. His commitment to helping individuals unlock their full potential is not just professional but deeply personal. This book is a culmination of his dedication to empowering others and a testament to his belief in the extraordinary impact that positive affirmations can have on one's life.

We certainly need this today, more than ever. In a world inundated with negativity, self-doubt, and external pressures, the importance of cultivating a positive mindset cannot be overstated. *Unstoppable Affirmations* is not just a book; it's a powerful resource on your journey toward greater growth and personal development.

Within its pages, you will find a blueprint for reshaping your thoughts, breaking free from limiting beliefs, and embracing a life of abundance.

This book is not a mere collection of words; it's a toolbox filled with affirmations meticulously crafted to address various aspects of your life. From shifting your mindset to overcoming obstacles, each affirmation is a stepping stone toward a more resilient, confident, and fulfilled you.

As you embark on this 31-day journey, know that you are not alone. The affirmations within these pages have the power to transcend words, reaching deep into the recesses of your mind and heart.

So, dear reader, prepare to unlock the potential of affirmations in your life. Commit to the daily practice outlined in this book, and watch as your thoughts, actions, and, ultimately, your life transform. My hope is that you will discover, as I have, how the words you speak can level up your life.

Here's to your journey of transformation, growth, and unstoppable success.

-Ruth Jones

Author of *Living the Sweet Life*
@ruthjonesinspires

INTRODUCTION

Level Up Your Life

I clearly recall, as a teenager, going on vacation and swimming in the ocean for the first time. Just before I plunged into the water, my mom warned me about rip currents—powerful currents that can pull even the strongest swimmers into turbulent waters. Much like the dangerous currents beneath the surface, our society is enveloped in the relentless pull of negativity threatening to drag us under. Media outlets are filled with narratives of violence, fatalities, and celebrity scandals, often highlighting the worst aspects of human behavior. Social media glorifies stories of struggle, comparison, conflict, and division. World events, wars, financial upheavals, and life's unexpected challenges contribute to daily uncertainty. Our brains are constantly bombarded with self-criticism, pessimism, fear, worry, anxiety, and other negative thoughts. It's no wonder mental health is at a critical, if not crisis, level in our culture. And if the external rip currents of negativity weren't enough to battle, our brains are internally wired for negativity, a phenomenon known as "negativity bias."

Negativity bias refers to our mind's inherent tendency to pay extra attention to negative stuff. We're more likely to remember and focus on bad things that happen than good things. Our minds have a built-in feature that spotlights the negative, making those moments stand out and stick around in our thoughts. Ever had a good day, but one negative thing happened, and when asked "how was your day," all you could think of was the one bad thing? That's negativity bias in action.

Our brain's negative default mode can lead us to live reactively and negatively, if left unchecked. As humans we often:

- Dwell on insults more than compliments and praise
- Remember the bad times better than the good ones
- Make decisions based on negative information rather than positive data
- Think about and react more strongly to negative events than equally positive ones

Let's face it, we are hardwired to think negatively. But it doesn't stop there. Negative thoughts lead to negative words. Research reveals that 70% of our self-talk is negative or self-critical. If we do nothing to break this pattern, eventually our negative words shape our actions, habits, and life outcomes.

But there is something that breaks the chain of negative thought patterns and rewires our mindsets and beliefs for success. Successful people, from entrepreneurs and top executives to Olympic athletes and best-selling authors, use this to achieve extraordinary results, and you can too–it's the tool of positive affirmations or what I call "unstoppable affirmations."

In this book, I will show you how to use affirmations to rewire limiting beliefs, transform your mind, and level up your life. In a world drowning in negativity, your journey to reclaim positivity begins here. If you're wanting more confidence, happiness, and success in life, this is the one technique that will supercharge your results. I can boldly say this because I've seen it work in my own life.

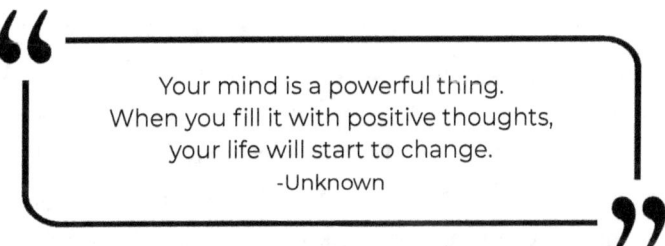

> Your mind is a powerful thing.
> When you fill it with positive thoughts,
> your life will start to change.
> -Unknown

How Affirmations Helped Change My Life's Trajectory

To truly grasp my profound connection with affirmations and the transformative power of speaking positive words over your life, I need to take you back to my early years. Growing up in the inner city of Detroit, at the age of 12, I had a secret: I was illiterate. Despite numerous attempts over the years working with tutors and being enrolled in expensive private schools, I still found reading to be a challenge and regularly received failing grades. To cope with the pressure and shame, I became quiet and withdrawn and even dabbled in drugs. My life was headed down the wrong path and fast.

In the seventh grade, my mother discovered and enrolled me in a community reading program that finally taught me how to read. Armed with this newfound ability, I still found myself with low self-esteem, failing grades, and behavior that matched. But one day I was reading in the Bible the story of David defeating Goliath, and I saw something I had never seen before. In the face of overwhelming odds, David spoke aloud a positive declaration of victory over his life. David said, paraphrasing: "I defeated a lion; I defeated a bear. This giant, in front of me, has no chance against the God I serve." David's words resonated with me. His ability to affirm his past victories before facing his giant inspired my first understanding of the power of words and self-encouragement.

This was the spark that changed my behavior for the better. I began to say things like, "If David can do it, I can do it;" "I can get better grades," and "I'm a leader, not a follower." As I spoke positive words over my life, my confidence grew, igniting my faith and empowering me to take action. Through prayer, determination, and affirming self-talk, I found the courage to turn my grades around and gained a new self-image. By the time I finished eighth grade, I stood as an award-winning honor roll student and recipient of the Spirit of Detroit Award for outstanding achievement and citizenship.

> The moment you accept responsibility for everything in your life is the moment you gain the power to change anything in your life.
> -Hal Elrod

A Teacher's Influence: Affirmations and Limitless Potential

When I got to high school, affirmations again showed up in another significant way impacting my life for the better. My beloved history teacher, Robert Lichtman understood the transformative impact of words. In his classroom, he had posters of positive affirmations all over the walls. He would start the day with having students share an affirmation with the class. As we sat there, speaking these positive words over ourselves and visually absorbing the affirmations covering the walls, he created an environment of positivity where we began to believe that anything was possible. His approach helped me realize that by speaking the right words over my life, I could level up my mindset and my life.

By the time I graduated high school, I held a 3.5 GPA and was in the National Honor Society, elected president of the student government, accepted into a Big Ten College, and awarded multiple scholarships. My newfound belief in my abilities empowered me to strive for everything I was capable of.

Had I not discovered the transformative effect of affirmations, I know the path I was on–struggling with shame, low self-esteem and dabbling in drugs–my story would likely have ended up very different. My journey exemplifies the life-changing potential of positive self-talk and our ability to shift our mindset, boost our self-esteem, and overcome negative beliefs and behaviors. Despite facing significant challenges, I refused to let my struggles define me and instead chose to believe in my potential for success. Using positive affirmations, you too can shift your mindset from one of fear and inadequacy to one of determination and possibility.

Empowering Your Journey: A Guide to Positive Transformation

Before I share with you all the exciting benefits of affirmations, let's cover some basics about what affirmations are and why they work.

What is an Affirmation?

Put simply, an affirmation is a positive, specific statement that affirms or declares something to be true. It is used to challenge negative, self-sabotaging, or unhelpful thoughts. An affirmation is designed to foster positive thinking and push you to achieve your greatest potential in life. It's also a tool for battling and replacing negative, limiting beliefs with positive, healthy ones. Affirmations serve as exercises for your brain, rewiring it to embrace positive truths. Through repetition, your thoughts, feelings, attitudes, and actions begin to align with these new beliefs.

Affirmations are a powerful tool to help you overcome all sorts of mindset, self-esteem, and personal growth issues. The affirmations in this book will effectively combat negative self-talk, low self-esteem and confidence, fear and anxiety, toxic thought patterns, stress, and motivation issues.

Why Affirmations Work?

Every day, the average person has around 60,000 thoughts, a significant portion of which, approximately 70%, tend to be negative. These negative thoughts eventually become negative words. These negative words give rise to anxiety and depression, creating a self-fulfilling prophecy where your words and beliefs shape your reality.

Science backs the connection between our mind and our mouth. Research on the brain found that one simple negative statement can have a ripple neurological effect by impacting the amygdala, causing it to release stress neurochemicals that drive you to make another negative statement – and many more (Newberg & Waldman, 2006). What if instead of speaking negative words and starting a negative neurological cycle, you instead intentionally chose positive, affirming words? You would change not only your brain for the better, but uplevel your belief system and accelerate your life's results!

Thanks to neuroscience research, it has been found that practicing self-affirmation boosts specific neural pathways (Cascio et al., 2016). In fact, affirmations are one of the most effective methods for rewiring negative thoughts and limiting beliefs and turning them into thoughts of positivity

A Look at the Research
The Science Behind Affirmations

- Affirmations have been shown to reduce stress and its deteriorating effects on your health (Sherman et al., 2009; Critcher & Dunning, 2015).

- Self-affirmations have been used effectively in interventions that led people to be more physically active (Cooke et al., 2014).

- Positive self-affirmations make it easier for us to accept messages and interventions that might otherwise feel threatening (Logel & Cohen, 2012).

- Affirmations can increase acceptance of unwelcome health-risk information and cause us to be more open to improving our health (Harris et al., 2007), such as eating more fruits and vegetables (Epton & Harris, 2008).

- Regular positive self-affirmations can be linked to better academic performance, especially for students who might feel left out (Layous et al., 2017).

- Affirming yourself positively has been proven to lower stress and reduce overthinking (Koole et al., 1999; Wiesenfeld et al., 2001).

- Affirming yourself can help you cope with uncertainty and improve your self-worth (Ruolei Gu et al., 2018).

and possibility. When you speak positive affirmations, not only are you reprogramming your *conscious mind*, which is responsible for your conscious actions and decisions, but more importantly, you are rewiring your *subconscious mind*, which shapes your behaviors and beliefs. Consider your subconscious a hidden filter on how you interpret and perceive the world.

The Bible echoes this in Proverbs 23:7 which says in part, *"For as he thinketh in his heart, so is he" (KJV)*. Ephesians 4:23 instructs us to *"be renewed in the spirit of your mind" (KJV)*. Change your thoughts, change your words. Change your words, change your life. Reprogramming your subconscious mind is vital to transforming your life, and it all begins with changing the way you talk to yourself.

Rewiring the Mind: From Self-Doubt to Empowered Thinking

When it comes to speaking affirmations, repetition and frequency are important. They work best when you do it a lot. Think of it like practicing a sport or playing a musical instrument. The more you do it, the better you get. Your thoughts are basically habits you've ingrained over time. So, if you want to change the way you think, you need to repeat positive affirmations regularly. It's like upgrading the software in your brain, swapping out old, unhelpful thoughts with new, empowering ones. When used consistently, this practice changes everything about how you perceive your life and the world.

> It's the repetition of affirmations that leads to belief. And once that belief becomes a deep conviction, things begin to happen.
> -Muhammad Ali

Consider a common fear like arachnophobia. By repeatedly telling yourself, "I'm scared of spiders," you reinforce this fear in your mind. Consequently, encountering a spider triggers a fear response because you've conditioned your brain to react this way. Negative self-talk, such as "I'm not good enough," or "I'll never achieve this goal," follows a similar pattern. These thoughts, when reinforced, become ingrained in your thinking, affecting your self-esteem, resilience, and motivation.

To break free from this cycle of negativity, we must replace these damaging thoughts with positive affirmations and practice them consistently. By repeatedly affirming positive beliefs, we can rewire our brains, forming new neural pathways that prioritize positive thinking. While it might seem strange at first, embracing positive affirmations is a scientifically proven method to reshape our mindset and live a more positive and empowered life.

The Benefits of Using Affirmations

I wrote this book as a powerful resource to empower individuals dealing with daily challenges or struggles as well as those already successful, who want to exponentially increase their success. No matter where you are starting from, this resource is designed to support your journey towards significant growth and transformation. The chapters in this book, whether it's affirmations on spiritual growth, relationships, finances, or health, hold powerful words that once spoken will help you rewire your thinking, unlock your potential, and accelerate your results.

Here are ten ways the affirmations in this book will help you level up your life.

1. Shift your mindset from negative to positive – Affirmations help guide you to a positive mindset, steering you away from damaging self-beliefs and drowning out the voices that say you're not enough. Shed the shackles of shame, comparison, inferiority, and envy. Reprogram your mind to embrace your unique identity, strengths, and abilities.

2. Boost your confidence and self-esteem – Think of affirmations like your daily pep talk. They're the positive vibes you send yourself, creating a foundation of self-assurance and a real sense of your own awesomeness.

3. Overcome limiting beliefs and behaviors – Ever feel held back by your own thoughts? Affirmations are your power tool to smash through those mental roadblocks and kick limiting beliefs to the curb, proving to yourself that you're capable of way more than you think.

4. Stop negative thoughts or self-doubt holding you back – Picture affirmations as your shield against the negativity monster. They're your way of saying, "Not today!" to those thoughts that try to hold you back.

5. Stay focused on positive change – Affirmations keep your eyes on the positive prize. They're like a compass pointing you toward the good stuff. Affirmations are your daily reminder to focus on the positive changes you want to see, helping you stay on track toward a brighter future.

6. Control your subconscious thoughts – Affirmations are like those catchy songs you can't get out of your head—except they're positive messages. They sneak into your subconscious and make it a positive place. You end up more optimistic and ready for whatever life throws your way.

7. Enhance your emotional well being – Affirmations create a nurturing space for self-love and acceptance, fostering a more positive emotional state and reducing stress levels.

8. Gain a healthy and optimistic outlook on life – Affirmations are like a daily dose of empowerment. By affirming your strengths and capabilities, you cultivate a sense of personal empowerment. Consistent use of affirmations trains your mind to adopt a positive perspective. This optimistic outlook not only shapes your response to daily challenges but also contributes to an overall positive approach to life.

9. Develop resilience in the face of challenges – Positive affirmations act as a secret weapon in building resilience. By regularly affirming your ability to overcome obstacles, you develop a mindset that embraces challenges as opportunities for growth, helping you bounce back stronger from setbacks.

10. Feel happier, healthier, and full of positivity – Through the use of positive affirmations you can consistently improve your health, promote healing in your body and mind, and move toward daily happiness.

>
> Affirmations are our mental vitamins, providing the supplementary positive thoughts we need to balance the barrage of negative events and thoughts we experience daily.
> -Tia Walker

While the benefits of using affirmations are numerous, I want to share with you a word of caution so that you have a balanced perspective on when to use affirmations and when to seek more serious help. Research supports the effectiveness of positive affirmations in helping individuals cope with challenging emotions and even combat thoughts of self-harm; however, it's important to acknowledge that affirmations aren't a cure-all. They should not be used to sidestep or ignore genuine issues, whether your own or those of others. Instead, they serve as a complementary practice, enhancing emotional well-being and motivation. When facing the overwhelming complexities of depression or any other significant challenge, in such circumstances, I highly recommend seeking support from a therapist, psychiatrist, or your local pastor.

Should Christians Use Affirmations?

Now, let's dive into a question I'm often asked, are positive affirmations biblical or do they belong in a Christian's life? Here are four principles that can help you understand the boundaries and safeguards for using affirmations in a biblically correct way.

1. Understand that the Bible has a lot to say about the words we speak and the power of our words. Here are just a few mentions of the power behind the words we speak:

Wise words bring many benefits. -Proverbs 12:14 (NLT)

The words of the reckless pierce like swords, but the tongue of the wise brings healing. -Proverbs 12:18

The tongue has the power of life and death, and those who love it will eat its fruit. -Proverbs 18:21

For the mouth speaks what the heart is full of. A good man brings good things out of the good stored up in him, and an evil man brings evil things out of the evil stored up in him. But I tell you that everyone will have to give account on the day of judgment for every empty word they have spoken. For by your words you will be acquitted, and by your words you will be condemned." -Matthew 12:34b-37

2. Positive affirmations must align with biblical truth. Affirmations that contradict the nature and laws God asks us to follow in scripture or affirmations that are contrary to God's desires are wrong and do not belong in a Christians life. The Bible is our standard of truth, and in this book, you will find only affirmations that align with God's word.

3. With affirmations, you must understand that the source of power must be God and not of ourselves. New age and humanistic affirmations focus on self as the source of power and the law of attraction as the means of attainment. As a believer, I want to make one thing clear. While positive thoughts and words hold power, our faith is not solely in them for success. Our trust is in God alone, His validation, and His desire for us to succeed, which is far greater. Positive affirmations that are based solely on our strengths, personal discipline, and abilities alone are not sufficient. The source and power of our affirmations must be God's strength and not our own.

4. It's possible to use affirmations that are neutral, not explicitly centered on Biblical themes but do not go against scripture teachings. Theologically termed "adiaphora," these are actions the Bible neither explicitly approves nor condemns. Here are some general positive affirmations that fit within this scope:

- I am diligent and effective.
- Today is going to be an amazing day.
- I focus on positive momentum.
- I embrace new opportunities.

Comprehending these four guiding principles will help you understand that speaking positive affirmations does have a place in a believer's life. Affirmations are a tool that can be used to help us grow in our confidence and personal development. But like anything else, affirmations should never be a substitute for authentic spiritual development. And when you learn to combine the practice of affirmations with memorization and declaration of Bible scriptures you magnify the power of what you say, even greater, which is why I have another book in this series that focuses on the power of scripture declarations.

How to Maximize This Book

I promise you, if you put your words to work using the affirmations in this book you will enjoy a more positive, successful, and loving life. Don't delay! Success begins with immediate and intentional actions. Let's get started on reprogramming your mind for success RIGHT NOW!

The book you hold in your hands makes it easier than ever to intentionally focus on positive words and see the benefits of reprogramming negative thoughts. The affirmations you're about to read have proven results. Each chapter is filled with life-giving, powerful words that are easy to complete in just a few minutes each day. That's why I created 31 of them. I encourage you to speak aloud at least one set of affirmations each day. Here are some quick tips on how to get the most out out of this book:

- Keep the book accessible so you can easily pull it out when you need a moment of mindfulness and positivity. Toss it in your glove compartment, gym bag or keep it on the

nightstand. Use the ebook on your phone so you can read them on the go.
- You can even transfer the affirmations to sticky notes where you can keep them visible so you can look at them throughout the day.
- Try memorizing your favorites so you can easily recite them to yourself in clutch moments.
- Use them repetitively. Repeatedly speaking these affirmations over and over reprograms your mental computer, enhancing your capacity to achieve more success, abundance, peace, health, and happiness.
- Incorporate these affirmations into your daily routine so that it becomes a habit. These affirmations are great to read first thing in the morning to set the right mindset, before bed to end your day with positive intention, on a commute or a coffee break, at the gym, or any time you need a daily dose of inspiration. I like to think of it as self-care at your fingertips!

Incorporating affirmations into your daily routine has the power to be truly life-changing. When you believe in yourself, you are more likely to take risks, persist through setbacks, and ultimately achieve success. Are you ready to become unstoppable? Then, dive into Chapter 1 right now to harness the transformative power of affirmations, unlocking your full potential to live your best life.

Affirmations to Level Up Your Spirit and Soul

DAY 1

Affirmations to Grow Spiritually

Spiritual growth consists most in the growth
of the root, which is out of sight.
-Matthew Henry

Spiritual development is not an accomplishment but
a way of life. It is an orientation that brings its own rewards,
and what is important is the direction of one's motives.
-David R. Hawkins

I am fearfully and wonderfully made.

I am a child of God, and I am surrounded by His love.

I am with God, and God is always with me.

I delight in the Word of God, and I meditate on it day and night, allowing it to guide and transform my life.

My life is a wonderful gift, and I am worthy of God's promises.

My heart will not be troubled or afraid. God has given me peace.

God renews my strength, and I have the endurance to keep going.

I have faith in God, and He loves me unconditionally.

Through God's help, I walk in power, love, and self-discipline.

I yield myself to God's will.

I trust in God with all my heart and lean not on my own understanding, acknowledging Him in all my ways.

God generously gives me wisdom as I ask for it.

God's Word helps me develop morals and uphold ethical values.

God has created me uniquely, and He knows me by name.

God has created me for a purpose, and I will find and fulfill it.

The peace of God rules in my heart.

The love of God flows through me. I am His, and He is mine.

I cultivate a spirit of gratitude, giving thanks to God in all circumstances and recognizing His daily faithfulness and love.

I am thankful, and I accept God's goodness in my life.

I am open to all opportunities and blessings that God sends my way.

I am led by God and trust in His guidance and divine wisdom.

I am made strong by God, and I do not need to fear.

As I wait on God, my power is renewed.

As I seek God, He hears me and delivers me from all my fears.

I am strong in Him and in His mighty power.

I am totally healed—physically, mentally, emotionally, and spiritually.

I will release doubt and fear and trust fully in God.

I will fulfill the purpose that God has for my life.

I am a vessel of God's love, and I extend kindness, compassion, and forgiveness to others.

God is for me and doing a good work in me.

I can walk confidently today because God's love is for me.

God is fighting my battles, and I will be victorious.

God has my back, and I am strong because of Him.

I walk in miracles beyond my expectations.

I accept everything that God has to offer me.

I let go of fear and embrace God's will for my life knowing everything will work out according to His perfect will.

I humbly surrender my will to God's will, seeking His guidance and direction in every aspect of my life.

I choose to see my difficulties as opportunities to grow closer to God.

I choose faith over fear.

I practice forgiveness towards myself and others, freeing my heart from resentment and anger.

I surrender my anxieties and worries to God, knowing that He cares for me and will provide for my needs.

I have a sound mind and an obedient heart.

I reject thoughts of fear, doubt, and negativity, replacing them with the truth of God's promises.

I embrace the power of prayer, knowing that it has the ability to move mountains and bring about miracles.

My strength comes from God, and He helps me do the impossible.

My steps are ordered by God, and I believe He has a purpose and plan for every season of my life.

DAY 2

Affirmations to Increase Self-Love

Your words have so much power. Every day, if you tell yourself, 'I love you,' if you give yourself one word of validation, it will change your mind.
-Ashley Graham

…'Love your neighbor as yourself.'
-Matthew 22:39

I am worthy of loving myself.

I am loved.

I am loving and lovable.

I love myself unconditionally.

I love and approve of myself.

I love myself. I love my body. I love my mind.

I love who I am inside and out.

I appreciate myself. I accept myself. I forgive myself.

I love myself more and more each passing day.

I am worthy.

I am creative.

I am strong.

I am wanted.

I am enough.

I am beautiful.

I am blessed.

I am okay.

I am my own hero.

I fearlessly follow my dreams.

I feel great about who I am.

I feel joyful to look at how far I've come.

I feel comfortable speaking my mind.

I am worthy of happiness and love.

I am perfect just the way I am.

I am in control of myself, and I am in control of my life.

I am creative and flexible, and I go with the flow of life.

I am unaffected by the judgment of others.

I am proud of my accomplishments.

I am not the anxiety attacking me; I am not what fears tries to tell me I am.

I am becoming the best version of myself.

I am grateful for the amazing, wonderful things in my life.

I am worthy of all the abundance, love, and amazing experiences I want.

I am unlike anyone else, and that is my best gift.

I am so grateful for this life.

I am doing the best that I can.

I am a force that the world needs.

I am optimistic and positive.

I am courageous and outgoing.

My worth is not determined by others.

I am responsible. I am independent. I am capable.

I am capable of achieving everything I want.

I am confident and intelligent.

My life is amazing.

My life is abundant.

My life is a blessing.

My life is rewarding and filled with joy.

My life is full of adventure and incredible experiences.

My space and boundaries are important.

I have unlimited power.

I have unique ideas to share with the world.

I have the ability to reclaim my power.

I have great potential that I tap into every day.

I have a special gift that the world needs—that the world deserves to see.

I trust myself.

I trust that things are going to work out for my good.

I am worthy of positive experiences and blessings.

I deserve to fill this space.

I deserve good things. I deserve happiness and joy.

I fully accept who I am, even as I better myself.

I release self-criticism and choose self-love.

I believe in myself and my abilities.

I treat myself with respect and honor.

I view myself through kind eyes.

I expect the best for myself.

I learn and grow every day.

I matter. My life matters.

I can achieve anything I put my mind to.

I naturally feel good about myself.

I easily forgive others.

I do my best every day.

I contribute my ideas and thoughts easily.

I know myself, and I honor my boundaries.

I promise to be kind to myself.

I choose to forgive myself rather than judge myself.

I don't need anyone else's approval to love myself.

I promise to be kind to myself because I deserve such kindness.

I accept and embrace myself for who I am.

I make a difference in the world.

I know others look up to me.

I appreciate that others love me for who I am.

I accept that others value my skills and knowledge.

It is in my power to choose happiness and love myself.

DAY 3

Affirmations to Increase Self-Esteem and Self-Worth

The strongest factor for success is self-esteem: Believing you can do it, believing you deserve it, and believing you will get it.
-John Assaraf

Not one drop of my self-worth
depends on your acceptance of me.
-Quincy Jones

I am worthy.

I am worthy of love and happiness.

I am unique and amazing.

I am powerful and resilient.

I am lovable and valued.

I am whole and complete.

I am my own best friend.

I am not my mistakes or my flaws.

I am becoming the best version of myself.

I am one-of-a-kind and no one can replace me.

I believe in my ability to express my true self with ease.

I believe in my ability to overcome setbacks.

I have the power to create the life I want.

I have everything I need to succeed.

I deserve to be successful.

I deserve everything good that comes to me.

I am worthy and my worth isn't affected by someone else's opinion.

I am beautiful, smart, and fun.

I am a valuable and important person.

There's absolutely nothing out of my reach.

Life is beautiful, and I am grateful for all I have.

I have many good qualities.

I have self-worth and inner beauty.

I have the power to be who I want to be.

I have limitless potential.

My voice and ideas are important.

My feelings and needs are important.

My self-worth doesn't depend on how others see me.

My failures do not define me; they simply help me grow and learn.

I respect myself, and others appreciate me.

I trust in my abilities.

I do not need to compare myself to others.

I forgive myself for things I have done in the past.

I follow my dreams no matter what.

I know who I am, and I release the thoughts that don't serve me.

I practice self-compassion when I make mistakes.

I like who I am and who I am becoming.

The love I give myself is reflected in all areas of my life.

The more I practice loving myself, the more lovable I become.

The only approval I need for self-esteem is my own.

I am proud of myself.

I am a unique gift to the world.

I am good enough.

I am beautiful, intelligent, and full of life.

I am right where I am supposed to be.

I am empowered to have the things I seek.

I am comfortable in my own skin.

I deserve to treat myself, just because.

I deserve the compliments that I receive.

I deserve love and happiness.

Everything is possible for me.

Nothing can stop me from achieving my dreams.

Nothing is more influential than my belief in me.

I love myself and all my flaws.

I love myself more and more each day.

I love and accept myself exactly as I am.

I love my personality and as I learn and grow, I love it even more.

I am a happy and successful person.

I am supported and loved by others.

I am loved even when people don't share my dreams.

I am surrounded by grace and positivity.

I am creative, strong, powerful, brave, and inspired.

My mind is filled with loving thoughts.

My life is a miracle, and I belong here.

I treat my body with love and care.

I don't have to be good at something to enjoy it.

I don't need to overthink this. I let go of things that are out of my control.

People value my work, my time, and my love.

I am brave and strong.

I am grateful for my life.

I am thankful for my body, mind, and spirit.

I am growing for myself.

I can achieve anything I want in life.

I can assert myself and stand up for myself and others.

I value the effort and work I put into all aspects of my life.

I accept myself unconditionally.

I prioritize myself and my needs.

I make time to care for myself.

I choose to view my life positively.

I let go of my past and live in the present.

DAY 4

Affirmations to Overcome Negative Thoughts

Once you replace negative thoughts with positive ones, you'll start having positive results.
-Willie Nelson

A pessimist sees the difficulty in every opportunity; an optimist sees the opportunity in every difficulty.
-Winston Churchill

I am not my emotions or my thoughts.

I am strong in mind, body, and spirit.

I am enough, and that's all that matters.

I am enough. I don't need to be perfect.

I am filled with positivity.

I train my mind to think optimistically.

I am in full control of my life.

I can control my thoughts, so I choose positive ones.

I give myself room to fail.

I give myself room to heal.

I give myself room to grow.

I give myself room to succeed.

I give myself room to thrive.

I love and approve of myself.

I love myself despite my thoughts.

I have faith in myself.

I have faith in my abilities.

I have the power to make the right choices for me.

I have made it this far, and I won't stop now.

I can do difficult things.

I can make a real difference.

I refuse to believe my own excuses.

I abandon old habits and choose new, positive ones.

I abandon all toxic thoughts.

Nothing is impossible, and life is great.

The world is full of possibilities.

Life is worth living despite my pain and sadness.

Obstacles are now falling away easily.

Today is a clean slate.

Success is mine.

I give myself permission to be me.

I give myself permission to be human.

I am bigger than fear. Fear does not define me.

I am filled with positive actions.

I am not afraid of failures and hardships.

I am delighted and content to have this life.

I am positive and will remain positive about my life.

I am in charge of my life and my happiness.

I am here with a purpose.

I am a miracle in motion.

I am blessed to see today. Every day is a gift.

I will not replay situations in my mind that upset or hurt me.

I will not become angry over things I cannot control.

I will survive this.

I will overcome these obstacles in front of me.

I will wake up tomorrow and do the best I can.

I choose happiness over sadness.

I release things that no longer serve me.

I release all thoughts that don't help me.

I release all negative thoughts.

I release the need to replay situations in my mind.

Thoughts can be changed.

Every thought I think is creating my future so I choose positive ones.

Toxic thoughts have no place in my life.

The past is over.

This darkness won't last forever.

Bad days will not last long if I remain strong.

I am much more than what I think I am.

I am loved and appreciated.

I am a talented person, and the world needs a talented person like me.

I am a work in progress.

I am self-sufficient and optimistic.

I am proud that I have come so far.
I am proud of all the hard days I have survived.
I am strong and can overcome anything in life.
I am tough. I will not give up on my life.
I am at peace with imperfection.
I am more than what people think I am.
I am gorgeous inside and out.
I welcome positivity into my life.
I welcome health and happiness.
I don't fear consequences.
I deserve everything good.
I deserve love, joy, and happiness.
I don't have to be productive to see value in myself.
I overcome all obstacles and challenges in my life.
I shine brighter after dark days.
I forgive myself for past mistakes I have made.
I forgive myself and let go of shame and blame.
I forgive myself and set myself free.
I focus on ways I can help myself get better.
My possibilities and capabilities are endless.
My life is a gift and it keeps on giving.
I forgive myself and release my worries to God.
I let go of impatience and trust in God's plan.
God wants what's best for me.

DAY 5

Affirmations to Let Go of Stress, Worry, and Anxiety

It's not the load that breaks you down, it's the way you carry it.
-Lou Holtz

Stress is caused by your thoughts, not the situation.
-Unknown

I am not my anxiety.

I am free from stress.

I am able to let go of anxiety and worry.

I am letting go of all my worries and fears.

I am able to release negativity and let go of stress.

I let go of all negative emotions.

I am in control of my mind and will become focused and worry-free.

I release any tension in my body from stress.

I release worst-case scenario thinking.

I don't need to worry about things I can't control.

I have the strength to move beyond my anxiety.

I have the power to overcome my doubts, worries, and fears.

I have the power to make all the necessary changes I need in my life.

Challenges are opportunities for me to grow.

This situation will pass. Everything is temporary.

Today, I'll do the best that I can.

I don't judge myself.

I release the past.

I free myself from what doesn't serve me or value me.

I will not only survive, I will thrive.

I overcome any obstacles in my way.

I will not be held back by worry and negative thoughts.

This stressful experience does not define who I am.

This feeling and situation is temporary.

I am far stronger than I realize.

I am able to overcome anything in my life.

I am safe and supported.

I am right where I need to be.

I am calm and full of joy.

I am releasing all negative emotions from my life.

I am a positive person who brings positive things into my life.

I know my worth is high.

I deserve a peaceful and loving life.

I have nothing to be anxious about.

I free myself from fear of the unknown.

I will not worry about money.

I take things one step at a time.

Today, and every day, I choose joy.

Releasing stress is easy.

I give myself space to be free.

I choose to think positive, nurturing thoughts.

I know that constant worrying is not helping to improve the outcome.

I focus my energy on my values, not my anxiety.

I have the ability to re-evaluate and overcome this stressful situation.

I accept and love myself unconditionally.

Affirmations to Level Up Your Health and Wellness

DAY 6

Affirmations for Health, Healing, and Wellness

A healthy outside starts with a healthy inside.
-Robert Urich

Happiness is an inside job. Don't assign anyone else that much power over your life.
-Mandy Hale

I am healed.

I am in great shape and continue to do the work to be so.

I am treating my body as a temple.

I am worthy, talented, deserving, and healthy.

I am healed of all heartbreaks and disappointments.

I do not hold grudges.

I let go of things that I cannot control.

I am healed of all emotional pain I feel.

I say yes to all things that support good healthy living.

I say no to things that do not serve me or my health.

I daily consume fresh, nourishing food from nature.

I love and care for my body.

I love myself unconditionally.

I love everything that has made me who I am.

I am worthy of all things wonderful.

I am worthy of good health.

I am allowed to feel good about myself.

I am not the negative thoughts that come to my mind.

I am getting healthier every day.

I am active.

I am thriving.

I am not a victim.

I am optimistic and secure.

I am at peace with everyone including myself.

My health and healing are my top priority.

My past does not define my present or my future.

My hardships bring me opportunities.

My life is a beautiful gift, and I respect it.

I allow myself to heal inside and out.

I overcome sad moments and bad days.

I release all emotional baggage.

I take time out for my mental health and sanity.

I create space to heal my broken heart and let go of the past.

I am thriving in my healing journey.

I am healthy and strong in my spirit, soul, and body.

I am healthy and wise and listen to the advice of my physicians.

I see myself as fully healthy, and I take action to be so.

My immune system is healthy and strong.

I am healed of all sickness, illness, and disease.

Water is good and gives life to my body.

Sunshine supports my health.

I get plenty of rest, and I sleep well.

I wake up rejuvenated and strong.

I prioritize exercise and physical fitness.

My muscles give me the support I need.

I have a healthy and pain-free body.

All my systems function perfectly—skeletal, muscular, nervous, circulatory, respiratory, digestive, urinary, lymphatic and reproductive.

I see myself at my highest and healthiest potential, and I am focused to get there.

I choose to be happy.

I am grateful for who I am and can be.

I am thankful to be alive today.

I am falling in love with taking care of myself.

I have a healthy body and a brilliant mind.

I deserve peace and mental well-being.

I accept my imperfections.

I feel loved and live in peace.

I give myself permission to heal.

I express my feelings respectfully.

I allow myself to rest when my body needs it.

I allow myself to give and receive love.

I treat myself with respect daily.

My life is filled with health and happiness.

There is no room for drama in my life.

The more I let go, the more freedom and healing I have.

DAY 7

Affirmations for Better Self-Care

Self-care is a priority and necessity, not a luxury.
-Unknown

Almost everything will work again if you unplug it
for a few minutes, including you.
-Anne Lamott

I am worth taking care of.

I am well-rested and full of energy.

I am powerful, healthy, and capable.

I am one-of-a-kind, and there is no one else like me.

I am worthy of love from myself and others.

I am investing in my future self.

I am overflowing with love, joy, happiness, and peace.

I make sure I get enough water.

I make sure I get enough exercise.

I deserve to treat myself well.

I deserve the best care.

I deserve the best and will not settle for anything less.

Taking care of myself is my first responsibility.

Taking care of myself brings me happiness.

Taking care of myself is loving.

Taking care of myself makes me smart.

I give myself permission to fail.

I give myself permission to succeed.

I give myself permission to release toxic thoughts.

I give myself permission to rest.

I enjoy my body and take good care of it.

I speak positively to myself.

I praise and encourage myself.

I stop myself from self-blame.

I am happy to be me.

I am relaxed and at peace.

I am what I need.

I am safe.

I am my biggest cheerleader.

I am worry-free.

I am getting better and better.

I am strong, unique, and smart.

I respect myself.

I care for myself daily.

I live my life without self-imposed limitations.

I release myself of any misery and suffering.

I release thoughts that drain me and refocus my energy on thoughts that empower me.

I will turn negative thoughts into positive ones.

I will not let negativity tear me down.

I will practice self-mercy and kindness.

I give myself grace.

I will take action and accomplish my goals.

I will try new things.

I will be kind to myself today.

I give myself proper nutrition.

I give myself time.

I give myself good vacations.

I take excellent care of myself.

I take care of my body, soul, and spirit.

I like myself, so I care for myself.

I always make sure to take care of myself first.

I will do my best for myself.

I accept myself for who I am.

Today, I will be better to myself than yesterday.

Today, I choose self-love instead of self-hatred.

I love myself, and I like myself too.

I love myself and the life I'm building.

I love myself for who I am, and my flaws are part of my perfection.

I push myself a little harder each day to reach my health goals.

I cheer myself on.

I have the power to make the right choices for me.

Toxic things and people have no place in my life.

It's ok for me to have fun.

It's okay for me to pamper myself.

It's okay for me to splurge on myself once in a while.

It's okay to feel good.

It's okay if things don't go as planned.

Healthy food fuels my body.

If I fail, I will fail forward.

The only person who can change me is me.

When I let go, I create space for something new or something better.

My life is a gift and I treat it accordingly.

My self-care is my priority, no matter how busy I am.

DAY 8

Affirmations for Better Mental Health

Mental health problems don't define who you are.
They are something you experience. You walk in the rain
and you feel the rain, but you are not the rain.
-Matt Haig

Your mental health is a priority. Your happiness is essential.
Your self-care is a necessity.
-Unknown

I am mentally strong.

I am mentally well and stable.

I am choosing to focus on my mental wellness.

I am capable of overcoming my mental health challenges and leading a happy life.

I am not my diagnosis.

I am healing.

I am in control.

I am tougher than the things that make life tough.

I am more than my trauma.

My mental health diagnosis and the challenges I face do not define me.

My anxious thoughts do not define me.

I fill my mind with positive thoughts.

I love myself unconditionally.

I love and approve of myself.

I have the strength to survive this.

I have coping skills to get through this crisis.

I have the final say in all of my emotions.

I release all of my worries.

I release tension from my body.

I release myself from stress.

I release toxic and negative thoughts.

I choose to react positively to all situations.

I choose to focus on the good.

Better mental health is possible for me.

Healing is possible for me.

Every day I am becoming a better version of myself.

One setback doesn't undo all that I have learned and accomplished.

I am in the process of actively healing my mental health for good.

I am doing the best I can.

I am happy to be me.

I am not ashamed of having anxiety.

I am in control of my mind.

I am in control of my life.

I accept the things I cannot control.

I am freeing myself from stress.

I can reach out to people who love me and get the support I need.

My loved ones look forward to when I reach out to them.

I prioritize and practice self-care.

I treat myself with compassion, kindness, and love.

I give energy to my solutions, not my problems.

I will not stress over things I cannot control.

I will not let my worries about tomorrow steal my peace today.

I will think only positive thoughts today.

I am strong, confident, and courageous.

I am thankful for the positive things in my life.

I am loved, wanted, and strong.

I am loved, important, and unique.

I allow myself to only be in healthy relationships.

My life is filled with miracles. My life is the greatest miracle of all.

I love what I see when I look in the mirror.

I love myself for who I am.

How I feel matters.

I deserve happiness.

I permit myself to take a mental health day to rest and recharge.

I take time to care for my spirit, soul, and body.

I value and prioritize my mental health as much as my physical health.

I can overcome anything with patience and practice.

I care about my mental health, and I am willing to put it before productivity.

I care for myself daily.

I believe in my ability to get through this.

I accept my flaws and find beauty within them.

There are people out there who will help me.

Reaching out for support is an act of strength.

I feel calm, safe, and peaceful inside.

This situation is challenging, but I will overcome it.

I face anxiety with courage and strength.

Anxiety is not who I am, and it does not control my life.

Depression is not who I am, and it does not control my life.

I control my thoughts—they don't control me.

I can overcome any stressful situation.

The panic and discomfort I feel are only temporary.

I take a deep breath, smile, and start again.

I am a child of God. My life is whole and complete.

DAY 9

Affirmations for Overcoming Depression

The best cure for worry, depression, melancholy, brooding,
is to go deliberately forth and try to lift with one's sympathy
the gloom of somebody else.
-Arnold Bennett

Sometimes, life will kick you around, but sooner or later,
you realize you're not just a survivor. You're a warrior,
and you're stronger than anything life throws your way.
-Brooke Davis

I am not my depression.

I am gaining strength every single day.

I am enough, and that is all that counts.

I am worth the time it will take to heal within.

I am a work in progress, and that's okay.

I am loved and appreciated even when it doesn't seem like it.

I am not less of a person because of how I feel.

I am much more than what I think I am.

I am not alone in this.

I can have a new beginning.

I can take this one day at a time.

I can overcome this moment and have a good day.
I can challenge negative thoughts with positive ones.
My life is beautiful.
My future is bright.
My feelings are real, but they don't define me.
My life has meaning.
I will gain strength every single day.
I will become a healthy and strong person.
I will experience joy and happiness again.
I will learn and grow through this difficulty.
I give myself permission to be free.
I give myself time to heal.
I trust in myself to continue to hope.
I am loved despite my sadness.
I am stronger than I realize.
I am needed regardless of how I feel.
I am valuable regardless of how I feel.
I am surrounded by love and support.
I am more than my trauma.
I am not broken.
I am not to blame for my depression.
I am capable of feeling good, positive, and content.
I am grateful to be alive.
I am here for a reason and a lifetime.
This discomfort won't last forever.
This feeling won't last forever.

This is only temporary.

These thoughts and feelings do not define me.

This sadness and depression does not define me.

This crisis will pass, and I will be okay.

I am resilient.

I am in the process of positive change.

I am worthy of happiness.

I am whole and complete.

I am not perfect, and that's okay.

I am more than my opinions of myself.

I am valued even when I'm not productive.

I am more than my depression.

I am in charge of how I feel, and today, I am choosing happiness.

I am learning more about how to handle my depression every day.

There is nothing wrong with me because I feel sad.

I'll have a great day today.

Life is an amazing gift.

It's okay to ask for help.

Asking for help with depression is how I show myself love.

Depression does not mean I am not loved or loving.

Depression is just a human condition, and I am only human.

Depression does not have the final word. I will be free.

I have made it this far, and I will not stop.

I have many gifts and talents.

I have many positive things in my life.

Nourishing myself is my top priority.

I love and accept myself unconditionally, especially on days like this.

I appreciate my life.

I value and respect myself.

I love my imperfections.

I forgive myself, and I don't blame myself.

I do my very best, and that's enough.

I take care of myself even when it's difficult.

I take another step toward positive change every day.

Every situation gives me an opportunity to learn and grow.

Every day is a gift, and I am blessed to see today.

I have God's strength in my weakness.

I trust in God to overcome this depression.

DAY 10

Affirmations for Improving Your Body Image

You have been criticizing yourself for years and it hasn't worked.
Try approving of yourself and see what happens.
-Louise Hay

Feeling beautiful has nothing to do with what you look like.
-Emma Watson

I am gorgeous inside and out.

I am worthy inside and out.

I am beautiful just as I am.

I am perfect and complete just the way I am.

I am worth celebrating.

My body is my home, and I choose to build it up instead of tearing it down.

My body is a gift. I treat it with love and respect.

My body is my best friend.

My body is wonderful, just as it is.

My body is a vessel for my awesomeness.

I love my body.

I love everything about my body.

I love how I look.

I love my teeth and my smile.

I love my beautiful hands and feet.

I love my hair just the way it is.

I love my waistline and shape.

I love my body at every stage of its journey.

I love me.

I don't need validation from others.

I feel beautiful in my skin.

I feel confident in my skin.

I do not compare my body to others.

I support others in their pursuit to feel positive about their body.

I accept all of me with love.

I strive to be healthy at any size.

Life does not begin at my goal weight. It's happening right now.

I am open to loving my body just as it is.

I am defined by who I am inside, not how I look.

I give myself permission to feel and look beautiful.

I treat my body with care and love.

I choose to think positively about myself.

I choose to love myself exactly as I am.

I like the person I am right now.

I have a loving relationship with my body.

I have no need to put anyone down to elevate myself.

I have no need to compare myself to magazine photos, which are airbrushed, photoshopped, and distorted.

I have the power to change anything I want.

I am allowed to take care of myself.

My body is a masterpiece.

My body supports me every day.

My body does not determine my worth.

My weight and age don't define me.

My very existence makes the world a better place.

My differences are what make me, me.

My body is always "beach ready."

My mind is a friend to my body, not a bully.

I honor my body.

It feels good to take care of my body.

Food doesn't have to be the enemy; it can be nurturing and healing.

This body makes things happen; this body is strong.

Other people's opinions about my body are irrelevant.

Being skinny or a certain body size is not my identity. I am identified by who I am on the inside.

I deserve to love my body today, not only after I reach my ideal weight.

No one has the power to make me feel bad about myself without my permission.

Loving my body is a demonstration of power.

There is more to life than worrying about my weight.

Aging is a privilege—I welcome the years with style and grace.

My changing body does not determine my confidence—how I feel does.

My brain is my sexiest body part.

I feel safe in my body.

Today, and every day, I am blessed.

I look exactly the way I'm supposed to because I was created in God's image.

DAY 11

Affirmations for Weight Loss

You didn't gain all your weight in one day;
you won't lose it in one day. Be patient with yourself.
-Jenna Wolfe

Weight loss doesn't begin in the gym with a dumbbell;
it starts in your head with a decision.
-Toni Sorenson

I am happy in my skin.

I am grateful for my body.

I am becoming the best version of myself.

I love myself no matter what my weight is.

I accept who I am, and I will not be defined by my weight or size.

I will always treat my body with the love, care, and appreciation it deserves.

I am on a lifelong path of wellness. Each day I commit to live my best life.

I am worthy of achieving my dream body.

I am worthy of a body I love.

I am capable of losing weight.

I am aware that losing weight takes time.

I am willing to put in the work required to lose weight.

I am excited to create a new relationship with food.

I am not ashamed to seek the advice of weight loss professionals to support my lifestyle change.

I will use all available resources to help me reach my weight loss goals.

I am ready to let go of old habits that no longer serve me.

My health is my priority.

My body appreciates how I take care of it.

My body is always working toward perfect health.

My body craves healthy, fresh, real food.

My weight loss process is tied to healthy foods and a healthier lifestyle not fad diets.

Unhealthy foods don't appeal to me.

Healthy weight loss is easy for me.

Being active fuels my body.

I am creating a body that I enjoy living in.

I am not what I eat; I am much more than that.

I am taking action steps every day to lose weight.

I am confident in my ability to lose weight.

I am setting realistic goals for my weight loss journey.

I am in control of my body, and losing weight is proof of this.

I am fit, healthy, and full of life.

I am active and full of energy.

My life is not consumed by a need to count calories.

My body is deserving of love and appreciation at any size.

My happy thoughts help create my healthy body.

I have been blessed with great physical health.

I have what it takes to achieve my ideal weight.

I will not give into temporary indulgence and triggered impulses.

I pause and evaluate before I give into cravings.

I have power over my food cravings.

I enjoy only the foods that are best for my body.

I make awesome choices for my health.

I take my own power back.

I celebrate my victories, no matter how small.

I forgive myself when I make mistakes on my weight loss journey.

I wake up each day with clear focus to reach my goal.

I choose to eat healthy foods that fuel my body.

I choose progress over perfection.

I eat only what my body needs, and I do not overeat.

I eat well, listen well, and live well.

I am a gorgeous person, inside and out. I do not need validation from others.

I feel good about myself.

I love and value myself.

I don't compare myself to others. Comparison is the thief of my joy.

I don't compare myself to others. Comparison is the enemy of my progress.

I don't compare myself to others. I'm on my own unique journey.

I don't compare myself to others. I'm busy working on myself.

I don't compare myself to others. I will shine like the sun in my due time.

I don't compare myself to others. I find complete satisfaction within.

Numbers on a scale don't determine my value.

Numbers on a scale don't define who I am.

I love my body today.

I make peace with my past and forgive my mistakes.

I release guilt connected to food or my past choices and decisions.

I surround myself with people who support my weight loss journey.

I enjoy living a healthy lifestyle.

Each time I resist temptation, I grow more disciplined.

I value self control.

I am capable of exercising.

I love being physically fit.

Exercise has become a part of my daily routine.

I exercise because it makes me feel good.

I deserve to feel and look healthy.

I enjoy eating foods that nourish my healthy body.

I enjoy every bite when I eat.

I recognize what's not working, and I make the changes needed.

I overcome all obstacles to reaching my ideal weight.

Every day I move closer to my ideal weight.

I am grateful for the weight I have lost.

When I look in the mirror, I see a healthy person.

I can. I will. I must.

Affirmations to Level Up Your Success and Abundance

DAY 12

Affirmations for Landing a New Job

A new job is an amazing chance to show the world
what you are capable of. You have everything to be great.
Just use it and never give up on your dreams.
-Unknown

Learn to balance your dream and your job
until your dream becomes your job.
-Unknown

I am worthy of a new job.

I am the best person for this job.

I am ready for career success and valuable opportunities.

I can find my dream job.

Everything always works out in my favor.

Every interview takes me closer to my dream job.

Every rejection moves me closer to my ideal job.

I am worthy of every opportunity that comes my way.

I am talented enough to receive a job that I love.

I am patient, and I know that I will find the right job for me.

I am going to find a career that makes me happy.

I am positive, confident, and happy.

I am ready for a new fulfilling job now.

My resume stands out and easily gets me an interview.

I am going to rock my next job interview.

I am ready for a constant stream of income.

Lots of new job opportunities are coming my way.

It's easy for me to find a new job that I love.

I only receive rewarding next-level offers that exceed my highest expectations.

The job search process is fun and easy for me.

I find it easy to network with others and make meaningful connections.

I am getting attention from recruiters every day.

I am committed to finding a new job that will be fulfilling and interesting.

I am confident that I have the right skill set to land the right job with exceptional pay.

I am confident that I will achieve success in my career.

I am open to an amazing position that will fulfill all my financial expectations.

I am worthy of receiving a job that I love.

I am open and receptive to all job opportunities.

I have what it takes to do well on my job interview.

I release my limiting beliefs over my career.

I am not afraid to put myself out there.

Employers are eagerly looking for me.

My skills are in high demand.

I'm one step closer to my dream job with every action I take.

I deserve to be paid well for my skills.

I will land a job with a great supervisor and team.

I trust God with all my heart for wonderful, new job opportunities.

DAY 13

Affirmations for Success at Work

Hard work beats talent when talent doesn't work hard.
-Tim Notke

Success is no accident. It is hard work, perseverance,
learning, studying, sacrifice and most of all,
love of what you are doing or learning to do.
-Pele

I am excellent at my job.

I am positive and optimistic.

I am grateful for my job.

I am free from stress.

I am flexible and willing to change.

I am a natural born leader.

I am willing to put in the work needed to achieve my professional goals.

I am consistent in my work. Every day I deliver something of value.

I am the author of my own success story.

My talents are valued and appreciated.

My presence makes a difference to my workplace.

My team is creative and inspires me to achieve success.

I sense love and support from my colleagues, mentors, and supervisors.

I take time throughout the day for breaks.

I use challenges to create new opportunities.

I choose to react positively to challenging situations.

I choose to give my smile freely and spread joy to those around me.

I give myself permission to go after what I want.

I let go of worries that drain my energy.

I enjoy being in my work space.

I look good, and I feel great.

Every day I am better than before.

People treat me with respect.

Success begins with my mindset, and I choose to remain positive.

It's okay to relax and reset after a long day.

Every mistake is an opportunity to learn.

It is okay to set boundaries when dealing with difficult people.

Pressure situations bring out the best in me.

Today, I leave all negativity behind me.

I will avoid office gossip and drama.

I will treat my colleagues with the same respect I want to be treated with.

I can hold my anger in check when stressful situations arise.

I will not stoop down to anyone's level.

I will have a positive impact on people around me.

I am thankful I have a job and a career path.

I am consciously pushing myself to develop in areas of my work.

I easily develop favor and rapport with everyone I work with.

I am successful in everything I do.

I am capable and equipped to handle anything that comes my way today.

I am surrounded and supported by smart, capable, and encouraging people.

I am surrounded by people who believe in me.

I am blessed to have a great team and healthy, supportive work culture.

I am a valuable asset to my organization.

I am confident to speak up, share my ideas, and ask questions to learn more.

I am proactive and get things done.

I am worthy of being paid highly for my time, skills, and effort.

My efforts at work are greatly rewarded. Promotion is my portion.

My past work experience has prepared me for this job.

I walk in a spirit of excellence.

I bring a positive attitude to work every day.

I spread light to those around me.

I avoid negative self-talk and self-sabotage.

I keep my work at work and maintain a healthy work-life balance.

My job does not define my worth or who I am.

I will transform failures into learning experiences.

I will go to bed earlier on workdays to ensure I perform at my full potential.

Today is a beautiful day.

I complete key tasks on time and within budget.

I embrace change and rise to new opportunities.

I believe in myself and have confidence in my abilities.

I have integrity when it comes to my work.

I have unique gifts and talents that are a perfect match for my position.

I have the humility to ask questions and receive the help I need.

I have the drive and motivation to pursue a promotion.

I have the confidence to delegate effectively and empower others.

I can succeed. I will succeed. I must succeed.

I can achieve anything with the help of my team.

I can influence others in a positive way.

I can transform obstacles into opportunities.

I am courageous to advocate and stand up for myself.

I am willing to learn, grow, and continuously develop.

I am going to have a productive work week.

I am ready and energized to perform at work.

Every day I deliver something of value.

I accept criticism as constructive feedback.

I receive all feedback with appreciation.

I treat everyone with respect, even when it's challenging to do.

I love change and easily adapt to new situations.

I have the perfect team of people to work with.

I will step out of my comfort zone.

I welcome the balance of work and self-care.

DAY 14

Affirmations for Promotion

People don't get promoted for doing their jobs really well.
They get promoted by demonstrating their potential to do more.
-Tara Jaye Frank

Some people want it to happen,
some wish it would happen, others make it happen.
-Michael Jordan

I am worthy and deserving of a promotion.

I am willing to do what it takes to be promoted.

I am skilled enough to earn a promotion.

I am grateful for my current position, and open to new opportunities.

I have a great relationship with my colleagues as well as my boss.

I am going to be successful.

I am confident in my abilities.

I believe that I can make a difference.

I believe in myself and my ability to be promoted.

My job is my first business partner.

My promotion will provide me with great increase.

My company values me for who I am and my work.

I am well rewarded for the work I do.

I am ready to move up in my career.

I will be successful in a higher position.

I am capable of accomplishing anything I put my mind to.

I am willing to do what it takes to reach my goals.

The more I learn, the more successful I can be.

I bring innovative ideas and fresh perspectives to my job.

I bring a lot to the table when it comes to my job.

I put out my best work effort, and I am rewarded in multiple ways.

I am ready for a promotion.

I am deserving of a promotion.

I am a perfect match for this promotion.

I won't quit until I get promoted or find a better job.

There are lots of great opportunities open to me.

I will rise and take action now.

Thank you God for blessing the work of my hands.

DAY 15

Affirmations for Abundance and Prosperity

There are many roads to prosperity, but one must be taken.
Inaction leads nowhere.
-Robert Zoellick

If you want to be financially free, you need
to become a different person than you are today
and let go of whatever has held you back in the past.
-Robert Kiyosaki

I am the creator of generational wealth.

I am a generational curse breaker.

I am worthy of a future full of prosperity.

Abundance is my birthright.

All of my actions lead to abundance and prosperity.

All my thoughts lead to diligence and plenty.

All resistance to money is gone from my life.

All the time I dedicate to my dreams is going to pay off.

I am worthy of the wealth I desire.

I am capable of achieving success.

I can overcome any financial obstacles.

I am an excellent money manager.

I am blessed and highly favored.

I am generous with my money.

I am a great giver and an excellent receiver.

I am a channel for money to flow to and through.

I am at peace with having a lot of money.

I am prosperous and successful in all that I do.

I have knowledge and understanding of money and making money.

I am financially free and debt free.

I am capable of success and wealth.

I have whatever I need to succeed.

I have more than enough to meet all my needs and desires and to be a blessing.

I have all that I need, and I generously share my success with others.

I have peace beyond understanding, and I walk in all abundance designed for me.

I have an abundant mindset.

I release negative thoughts about money.

I am prosperous, and I will continue to be prosperous.

I leave an inheritance for generations to come.

I am thankful for abundance and prosperity coming to pass in my life.

I am confident in all that I am, all that I have, and all that I can do.

I am willing and able to create wealth.

I am making financial progress.

I am worthy of wealth and able to enjoy it.

My dreams will come true.

My income is always increasing.

My giving is always increasing.

My actions create constant wealth.

My life is full of wealth opportunities.

My current circumstances do not affect my desired reality. I stay focused on the life I want.

My life will not revolve around money, because I am secure.

I possess money, but money does not possess me.

I look for wise investment opportunities and ways to bless others financially.

I give generously and even more is given back to me.

My financial freedom is within reach.

I make money doing what I love.

I am patient in building wealth and never resort to get-rich-quick schemes.

I achieve my financial goals.

I accept and receive unexpected money.

I spend money wisely and with a purpose.

I live from a place of abundance.

I boldly conquer my money goals.

I see wealth opportunities everywhere.

I release all resistance to wealth.

I create prosperity easily and effortlessly.

I always have enough money.

I give myself permission to be wealthy and successful.

I receive prosperous ideas and act on them with ease.

I openly share the wealth I receive.

I embrace new avenues of income.

I am a wise steward with money.

I am skilled at making passive income and maximize multiple channels for increase.

I educate myself to know how to handle money well.

I deserve to make more money.

I see myself living in limitless abundance.

Money comes to me in abundance in expected and unexpected ways.

Money creates a positive impact on my life.

There is a clear path before me to abundance.

Favorable circumstances await me. I am excited to receive them.

Yes, my finances are secure, and they will continue to grow with ease.

Everything I want is on its way to me in due time.

Opportunities are coming and will continue to come to me.

Everything I need to succeed is already within me.

All things work out for my good.

It's never too late to turn my dreams into reality.

I focus on ways to make a lot of money easily.

I honor God with all my income.

I am a willing vessel God uses to spread love, kindness, and abundant generosity.

I open my heart to accept all the abundance God has for me.

I wake up peacefully, knowing that God is taking care of me.

God has blessed me with the ability to attain wealth through my skill set.

DAY 16

Affirmations for Entrepreneurial Success

The best way to predict the future is to create it.
-Peter Drucker

What do you need to start a business? Three simple things: know your product better than anyone, know your customer, and have a burning desire to succeed.
-Dave Thomas

I am an entrepreneur.

I am successful.

I am confident in my brand and mission.

I am confident in my ability to create wealth.

I am highly successful and passionate at what I do.

I am great at solving people's pain points and offering them solutions of great value.

I am serving my life's purpose through my business.

I am increasingly confident in my ability to create the life I desire.

My ideas generate wealth and prosperity.

My brand is clear, authentic, and powerful.

My expertise and hard work earn me great profits.

My work makes a positive difference.

My potential is limitless.

I learn as I go.

I can and I will do this. Nothing can stop me.

I turn my expertise into income.

I focus my energy on what I'm good at.

The more I give, the more I receive.

The right mentors help me excel in reaching my entrepreneurship goals.

There are no limits to what I can achieve.

This does not need to be perfect.

This is going to be a great day.

I am worthy of my dreams and goals.

I am creating a life I deserve to live.

I am committed to doubling my income and beyond.

I am 100% committed to my success.

I am a powerful creator.

I am in charge of my efforts and success.

I am capable and confident in running a successful, prosperous business.

I am inspired and motivated.

I am always striving for progress, not perfection.

I got this.

I offer the best product/service that money can buy.

I believe in myself and my abilities.

I believe I can achieve greatness.

I give up my limiting beliefs on money.

I give myself permission to become wealthy.

Entrepreneurship is a path of prosperity for me.

I am paid richly for my skills, services, and products.

All I need to do is take the next tiny step.

Self-doubt has no place in my life.

I reject all imposter syndrome.

Now is my time.

My goals are possible.

My business is flourishing.

My knowledge is profitable.

My income is constantly increasing.

My sacrifices are leading to prosperity and wealth.

I make a difference.

I make a positive impact in what I do.

I make tough decisions and do hard things when I have to.

I do not worry about the things I cannot control.

I release my doubts and insecurities.

I use my competition as inspiration.

I allow creativity to flow through me with ease.

I lead with integrity, passion, and care.

I see every setback as a chance to make a comeback.

I place no limits on the amount of money I can make.

I provide products and services that people need.

I have the ability to create absolutely anything I want.

I invest in myself and my business every day.

I deserve to be financially free.

I love what I do.

I establish a healthy work-life balance.

I create a wonderful life for me and my family.

I overcome hurdles and difficulties with ease.

I will not settle for less.

I accomplish my money goals this year.

Today, I am going to be better than yesterday.

When one door closes, another one opens for me.

Money flows into my business easily and effortlessly.

What I focus on grows, and so I focus on my business.

I am creating generational wealth.

I am persistent in all that I do.

I am getting closer to fulfilling my dreams.

I am building a powerful and positive business.

I am capable of creating success.

I am great at time management and people leadership.

I am learning and growing as an entrepreneur.

I am driven by passion and purpose.

I am worthy of financial security.

I receive my ideal customers/clients.

My clients/customers love my business and become raving fans.

I am worthy of success.

All my goals are coming to pass.

It's okay to take breaks and rest my body and mind.

It's ok to make mistakes, and I will not let them hinder me.

My dreams are becoming reality.

My actions create constant prosperity.

My business changes lives.

My business is a massive success.

I make money while I sleep.

I speak confidently about my business.

I create the life I want.

If it's to be, it begins with me.

I trust God to reward my efforts with success.

I step back and let God lead the way.

Affirmations to Level Up Your Attitude and Confidence

DAY 17

Affirmations to Believe in Yourself

Life has no limitations, except the ones you make.
-Les Brown

Believe in yourself! Have faith in your abilities!
Without a humble but reasonable confidence in your
own powers you cannot be successful or happy.
-Norman Vincent Peale

I am full of unlimited potential.

I am a strong and powerful person.

I am capable and confident.

I believe in myself and my ability to succeed.

I am ready for whatever the future holds.

I am releasing all my old fears.

I am great at what I do.

I am not my thoughts.

I am not my fears.

I am proud of myself for showing up.

I am safe. I am protected. I am loved.

I am not a prisoner of my mind. I control my day.

My challenges help me grow.

My gifts are unique and one-of-a-kind.

My thoughts are valuable.

My mistakes will not define me.

My contributions are meaningful, valued, and abundantly rewarded.

My voice and opinions are important.

My strength is greater than any struggle.

My body is my home, and I choose to build it up instead of tear it down.

I will be kind to myself.

I will not question myself.

I will not stop until I reach my goals.

I will accept whatever comes my way and overcome.

There are people in my corner who support me.

Every day I am creating a life I love.

Every day I nurture my body.

Every step I take gets me closer to my goals.

Every challenge is an opportunity to grow.

Every day is another chance to shine.

I am not my fears.

I am accepted here.

I am valuable.

I am trustworthy.

I am full of life.

I am allowed to take up space.

I am strong and resilient.

I am bigger than any obstacle.

I am allowed to be wherever I want to be.

I am grateful for how much I have grown.

I am grateful for all the good things in my life.

I am understanding of others and their circumstances.

I am abundant in kindness and love.

I am happy when I challenge myself.

I am completely supported, safe, and rooted in the present moment.

I can accomplish great things.

I can ask for and receive help from others.

I can face difficult challenges.

I can face every challenge.

I can express my true self.

I can have everything I want in life.

I choose to love myself exactly as I am.

I choose to not give in to fear.

I choose to be happy.

I choose courage over fear and peace over perfection.

I have the grace to love the broken parts of me and pursue healing.

I have unique and valuable gifts to offer the world.

I have the power to change my story.

I have the courage to be seen.

I am in complete control of my emotions.

I am bigger than my doubts.

I am bigger than my insecurities.

I am enough, just as I am.

I am radiant. I am stunning. I am beautiful.

I am engaging and welcomed when I enter a room.

I am growing into who I am supposed to be.

I am surrounded by positive people.

I am surrounded by uplifting, supportive people who believe in me.

I am able to ask for and accept help when I need it.

I am healthy and full of life.

I am always worthy. I matter.

I am willing to learn, grow, and change.

I thrive in everything I do.

I rise above all my insecurities.

I strongly believe in myself.

I empower and encourage everyone I know.

I celebrate my progress each and every day.

I accept compliments from others.

I love myself completely, flaws and all.

I forgive myself for my mistakes.

I deserve peace and well-being.

I speak to myself with loving-kindness.

I release all doubts and insecurities about myself.

I release fear and welcome faith.

I embrace the new me and let go of the old me.

I have all the tools for success.

I have the potential to achieve my dreams.

I have the power to make an impact on the world.

I receive solutions to all my problems.

I may make mistakes, but I am not my mistakes.

Mistakes do not define me.

I am focused on my journey.

I show compassion for myself in all situations.

I bring light to those around me.

I do not have to be perfect. I just have to show up.

I feel comfortable with my thoughts and feelings.

I feel protected and validated.

I already have everything I need for success.

It is safe for me to be my authentic self.

It's okay to step out of my comfort zone.

Nobody can make me feel small.

Success and abundance are my birthright.

The world will value my contributions.

In the face of fear and uncertainty, I choose gratitude and trust.

No matter what, I am always worthy of love, kindness, and respect.

DAY 18

Affirmations to Increase Confidence

Self-confidence is a super power.
Once you start to believe in yourself, magic starts happening.
-Oscar Auliq-Ice

Optimism is the faith that leads to achievement.
Nothing can be done without hope and confidence.
-Helen Keller

I am a confident person.

I am confident in my uniqueness.

I'm secure in who I am now and confident in who I am becoming.

I am my best source of motivation.

I am braver than I think.

I am stronger than I feel.

I am stronger than my fears.

I am stronger than my doubts.

Confidence is available to me now.

Confidence is possible for me now.

Confidence is mine.

I have all the confidence I need to tackle the day.

I have unshakable faith.

I have everything I need for success.

Every day I become a better version of myself.

Every day I grow more confident.

Everything is possible.

I can overcome any challenges.

I can overcome every obstacle that comes my way.

I embody confidence.

I see myself walking confidently into every situation.

I look forward to the future.

I deserve to feel good about myself.

I radiate self-confidence.

I shine bright like a diamond.

I am strong, confident, and courageous.

I am the master of my thoughts.

I am not afraid of the unknown.

It's okay to leave my comfort zone.

When I set my mind on something, I won't stop until I reach it.

There is nothing I am afraid of.

It's okay to fail because that's the road to success.

All I need to succeed is within me.

My confidence grows stronger every day.

Nobody has the right to make me feel worthless.

I am worthy of being confident.

I am aware of my unique gift to the world and share it freely.

AFFIRMATIONS TO INCREASE CONFIDENCE

I am a good person who deserves to be treated with love and respect.

I am compassionate with others and myself.

The more I let go, the better I feel.

The more I choose to be confident, the more confident I become.

My confidence is at the next level.

I can achieve everything I want.

I can let go of my insecurities.

I stand up for myself.

I will tackle the day ahead with confidence.

I handle stressful situations with confidence.

I release everything that doesn't serve me.

Challenges are opportunities to grow and improve.

What I want is already here or on its way.

There are no roadblocks I cannot overcome.

I am free of negative self-talk.

I am a positive person, aware of my full potential.

I am grateful for my journey and its lessons.

I am ready to step into the most confident version of myself.

I conquer all limiting beliefs.

My mood doesn't depend on other people's opinions.

I love to meet other people and make new friends.

I am creative and open to new solutions.

My happiness and well-being are important.

My confidence comes with practice.

I accept compliments easily.

I receive positive people into my life.

I make a difference by showing up every day and doing my best.

I fill my mind with positive thoughts.

I choose not to stay around negative people.

I don't have to waste time on people whose company I don't enjoy.

I believe in my abilities and express my true self with ease.

I am confident that God is on my side.

DAY 19

Affirmations to Overcome Fear

Everything you want is on the other side of fear.
-Jack Canfield

Thinking will not overcome fear but action will.
-W. Clement Stone

I am fearless.

I am courageous in all that I do.

I am always eager to try new things.

I am strong enough to overcome any fear in my life.

I easily go beyond the limitations of my ego.

I easily release all fear and worry.

I take action now.

I always take action without hesitation or fear.

I keep pushing until I succeed.

I accept challenges with enthusiasm and confidence.

I always succeed in spite of setbacks.

I breathe in confidence and breathe out all fear.

I choose to feel safe and secure at all times.

I commit myself to developing the highest level of fearlessness in my life.

I constantly strive to move beyond my fears.

I do the things I fear and take control of my life.

I face all my fears head on.

I let all worries and fears float away as I focus my mind on my strengths.

I am turning into someone who is naturally confident and fearless.

I push forward and leave every fear behind.

I put my fears into proper perspective and then continue with confidence.

I replace any thought of fear with faith.

I see my fears for what they are—lifeless thoughts that I no longer give power to.

I willingly release all fears and doubts as they arise.

I walk in love, power, and self-discipline.

I naturally persist when things get tough.

I face and conquer fear with swift, decisive action.

I feel totally at ease in front of a group of people.

I have all the strength I need to defeat my fears.

My dreams are much greater than my fears.

My mind is too full of optimism to harbor worries and fears.

Today, I give myself permission to be greater than my fears.

Today, I give myself permission to succeed in the face of doubt.

From now on, fear isn't an option.

I know that all is okay in my life.

I know that my future is secure.

I know that fear disappears when I do the thing I fear.

I know that my fears disappear when I act in spite of them.

I have a purpose and fear won't stop me from fulfilling it.

Every day I bravely expand my comfort zone.

Gaining strength from difficulty is something I do naturally and easily.

The more I face my fears, the weaker they become.

Being confident and courageous comes naturally to me.

Facing my fears empowers me to rise above them.

Fear is nothing more than an emotion, and I am greater than my emotions.

As I challenge my fears and doubts, I am strengthened and empowered.

As I challenge my fears, I release my need to dwell on them.

My faith in God empowers me to overcome any fear.

DAY 20

Affirmations to Become More Grateful and Thankful

When gratitude becomes your default setting, life changes.
-Nancy Leigh Demoss

When life is sweet, say thank you and celebrate.
And when life is bitter, say thank you and grow.
-Shauna Niequist

I am forever grateful.

I am grateful to be alive.

I am grateful for good health.

I am grateful for all the lessons I've learned.

I am grateful for what my mistakes have taught me.

I am grateful for the freedom to live my life as I like.

I am grateful for who I am and everything I am capable of.

My day begins and ends with gratitude.

Each and every day, I count my blessings.

I live in a state of gratitude, and I am always thankful.

I am thankful for everything in my life.

I am thankful to have a loving family.

I am thankful for every person who believes in me.

I am thankful for every person who supported me in some way.

I am thankful for every opportunity that comes to me.

I am thankful for all the doors that have opened for me.

I am thankful for my increasing income.

I am thankful for all the money I have in my bank accounts and investments.

I am thankful for all the finances I have to invest in my growth.

I am eternally grateful for all of the blessings I have in my life.

I am deeply grateful for the freedoms I enjoy.

I walk daily with an attitude of gratitude.

I give myself permission to be thankful regardless of my circumstances or emotions.

Gratitude changes my focus to the good in my life.

I am grateful for all the things in my life that bring me joy and happiness.

I am grateful for life's challenges for helping me grow and become who I am.

I am grateful for the abundance in my life.

I am grateful for everything–the good and the bad–because it developed me.

I am grateful for all the wonderful people in my life.

I am grateful for a roof over my head and a warm bed to sleep in.

I am grateful for the people that cross my path daily.

AFFIRMATIONS TO BECOME MORE GRATEFUL AND THANKFUL

I am grateful for my success.

I am grateful for my senses of taste, vision, hearing, touch, and smell.

I am grateful for my body and the health I have.

l am grateful for my relationships and the love and connection we share.

I might not say it every day, I am always grateful for the love I receive.

I am thankful to God for bringing to pass all the wonderful things in my life.

DAY 21

Affirmations to Take Personal Responsibility

When you blame others, you give your power away.
When you take responsibility, you take
your power back to transform your life.
-Unknown

If it's never our fault, we can't take responsibility for it.
If we can't take responsibility for it, we'll always be its victim.
-Richard Bach

I am responsible.

I am responsible for my attitude.

I am responsible for my feelings.

I am responsible for my own happiness.

I am responsible for my health.

I am responsible for my belief in myself.

I am responsible for my financial health.

I am responsible for my success.

I am responsible for everything in my life.

I respond with ability.

I take responsibility for my past.

I take responsibility for my present.

I take responsibility for my future.

I take responsibility now.

Taking responsibility for my life empowers me.

Being responsible is one of my core values.

Today, I take 100% responsibility for my life.

I wake up, clean up, and show up.

I stand up, shape up, and grow up.

I am turning into someone who is competent, responsible, and self-reliant.

I am free from the financial support from my parents, relatives, and friends.

I am willing to do whatever it takes.

I am responsible for learning and gaining the skills, tools, and resources to live a better life.

I take responsibility for who I am–the good and bad.

I take responsibility for my choices and decisions.

I take responsibility for my set-backs and come-backs.

I step fully into personal responsibility.

I stand on my own two feet.

I am stable and trustworthy.

I keep my word.

I manage my money effectively and responsibly.

I earn my own money.

I am confident and secure.

I take control of my own life.

I show compassion to others.

I find it easy to do things for myself.

AFFIRMATIONS TO TAKE PERSONAL RESPONSIBILITY

I accept responsibility for nurturing the gifts and strengths within me.

I accept responsibility for all of my choices.

I accept responsibility for my actions.

I choose to be accountable.

I support myself.

I use my time wisely and well.

I alone am responsible for how I act and react in any situation.

I am responsible for who I surround myself with.

I am responsible for what I allow from others.

I am responsible for what I accomplish in life.

I am responsible for the words that I speak.

I am responsible for my spending habits.

I am responsible for my daily habits.

I am responsible for my self-improvement.

I am responsible for nurturing my passions.

I am responsible for growing my spiritual walk.

I am responsible for growing in knowledge and increasing my understanding.

I am responsible for what I consume.

I am responsible for finding solutions to my problems.

I am responsible for all my thoughts, words, choices, and actions.

I take full responsibility for my life so that I may live my dreams.

Affirmations to Level Up Your Relationships and Family

DAY 22

Affirmations for Improving Your Relationship

A good relationship is when someone accepts your past, supports your present, and encourages your future.
-Zig Ziglar

A good relationship always creates an "Us" without destroying a "Me."
-Unknown

I am lovable and worthy of receiving love.

I am deserving of love just as I am.

I am committed to working on my relationship.

I am open to the advice and accountability of a relationship coach.

My partner makes me feel loved and safe.

My partner values me.

My partner trusts and respects me.

My partner loves me for who I am.

I believe in our relationship.

I believe in the integrity of my partner.

I release resentment towards my partner.

I release control in my relationship.

I appreciate our differences.

I allow my partner to be their authentic self.

I forgive myself for hurting my partner.

I take responsibility for my own emotions.

I create and stick to boundaries in my relationships.

When I love myself, my partner will love me back.

The more love I give, the more I receive.

We go out of our way to support each other.

It's okay for me to ask for what I need and desire in my relationship.

Our love grows stronger each day.

I am worthy of my partner's love and respect.

I am worthy of happiness in my relationship.

I am encouraged by my partner's love for me.

I am confident in our relationship.

I am confident that my partner makes wise choices.

I feel safe in my relationship.

I feel comfortable sharing my feelings and thoughts with my partner.

I feel free to be myself in my relationship.

I feel loved, cherished, and fulfilled in my relationship.

My partner and I are in a healthy relationship.

My partner and I are perfect matches for each other.

My partner and I support each other to become successful individuals.

My partner and I share a strong and healthy love for each other.

My partner and I resolve our conflicts respectfully and peacefully.

My partner and I are generous towards each other.

My partner and I always think the best of one another.

My partner accepts my flaws and helps me to become a better version of myself.

I am able to view things from my partner's perspective.

I am willing to listen.

I am open to receiving love.

I have faith in my relationship.

I am grateful for my relationship.

I enjoy having an amazing relationship.

My past does not define me and will not hinder my present relationship.

My trust is non-negotiable.

My needs in this relationship are important and valid.

My partner truly respects my boundaries, and I respect theirs.

My partner is happy being in a relationship with me.

My relationship is worth the effort.

My partner matters to me.

I will do something nice for my partner today.

I will communicate in a healthy and loving way.

I bring flirtation and playfulness to our relationship.

I make intentional, consistent efforts to be my best self in my relationship.

I trust my partner.

I forgive them easily.

I grow in my understanding of my partner.

I listen to my partner with an open heart and mind.

I love, respect, and validate my partner.

I speak highly and respectfully of my partner even when they are not around.

My partner appreciates me.

My partner compliments me often.

My partner and I communicate effectively, truthfully, and openly.

I give my relationship the time, attention, and effort it deserves.

I show appreciation for my partner every day.

I pray over my partner every day.

I am open to God's perfect will for the next chapter of our relationship.

DAY 23

Affirmations for Finding Love, Romance, and a Healthy Relationship

Love isn't about finding the perfect person. It's about realizing that an imperfect person can make your life perfect.
-Sam Keen

A healthy relationship will never require you to sacrifice your friends, your dreams, or your dignity.
-Dinkar Kalotra

I am worthy of love.

I am lovable and loved.

I am ready to receive love.

I am worthy of a healthy, loving relationship.

I am making room for an amazing relationship in my life.

I am capable and deserving of a lasting relationship.

I release my fears and embrace my future mate.

I am single, strong, and beautiful inside and out.

I am open to love and surrounded by love.

I am exactly where I am supposed to be.

I am enough for my mate just as I am.

I am attractive and desirable.

I am ready for commitment.

I am content, hopeful, and free from anxiety about finding true love.

I have hope and a future.

I receive a trusting and loving relationship.

My mate will be affectionate, loving, and romantic.

Dating and courtship is a joyful experience for me.

I love who I am, and so will my future mate.

I've done the work, and now I'm ready for love.

Loving myself allows me to love others.

It is safe for me to love and be loved.

The love of my life will be drawn to me.

I am handsome/beautiful and young at heart, and I express that from the inside out.

I am healed, whole, and ready to accept love.

I am capable of being in a healthy relationship.

I am making room for an amazing person to enter my life.

I am open and ready to find my true love.

I deserve to be loved and respected.

I deserve care and attention from someone special.

I release whatever is standing in the way of love.

I release any relationship trauma from my past.

I forgive myself for my past mistakes.

I say goodbye to the wrong relationships and say hello to true love.

I am open to healthy and loving relationships.

I let go of my need to control.

I can let my walls down and be vulnerable.

I will not resist anymore. I am open to a healthy and happy relationship.

I respect myself, and others respect me.

I love me for who I am, and so does my future mate.

My heart is open to receiving love.

My true self is loveable just as I am, right now.

My future mate will be my healthiest relationship.

My future mate will treasure me and protect me.

My future mate will be faithful to me and give of their time, treasure, heart, and attention.

My mate will come into my life at the right time.

My love life is a reflection of the love I have for myself.

What is meant for me will not pass me by.

I am single, and I am worth so much.

I deserve real and authentic love.

I welcome love into my life.

I will be a great blessing to my future mate.

I give and receive unconditional love.

I am patient in the process of receiving true love.

My future relationship will be healthy and lasting.

My future relationship will honor God.

I trust God to help me find true love.

God's timing for me is perfect.

I date/court confidently knowing that God cares for me and has my back.

I open my heart to God's love and trust that my mate's love will follow.

I choose to rejoice. God's mate for my life will be attracted to my spirit.

I step back and let God lead the way.

I will let God guide me to my mate and trust that He knows best.

DAY 24

Affirmations for a Great Marriage

What counts in making a happy marriage is not so much how compatible you are but how you deal with incompatibility.
-Leo Tolstoy

A good marriage is one which allows for change and growth in the individuals and in the way they express their love.
-Pearl S. Buck

I am blessed with a wonderful spouse.

I am absolutely committed to my spouse.

I am a better person because of my spouse.

I am happy and content in my marriage.

I am in a secure and loving marriage.

I am honest, trustworthy, and truthful.

I am thriving in my marriage.

I intentionally put in the work to make it last forever.

My marriage is becoming deeper, stronger, and more rewarding each day.

My marriage will stay strong for the rest of our lives.

My marriage is built on love, trust, and respect.

My marriage is full of love and abundance.

I love and find my spouse sexually desirable.

I love being in love and loved by my spouse.

I love making my spouse happy.

I love to flirt with my spouse.

I love kissing my spouse.

I love making love to my spouse.

I care about their needs.

I listen to my spouse with an open mind.

I make efforts to be my best self for my spouse.

I make time to show my appreciation for my spouse.

I value my spouse and they value me.

I verbalize my love for my spouse every day.

Our marriage is strong.

Our marriage is sizzling and passionate.

Our marriage brings out the best in us.

Our love life just gets better and better.

Our intimacy and passion increases day by day.

We grow closer emotionally and spiritually.

We complement each other.

We encourage each other.

We forgive each other.

Nothing can separate us.

Together, we can get through anything.

We are teammates, not competitors.

I am flexible in my marriage.

I am forgiving in my marriage.

I am patient with my spouse.

I am faithful to my spouse and my spouse is faithful to me.

My spouse is my top priority.

My spouse and I are extremely attracted to each other.

My spouse and I show each other physical affection.

My spouse and I make time for physical intimacy and satisfy each other's needs.

My spouse and I are emotionally intimate and transparent with each other.

My spouse and I love working together to create our dream life.

My spouse and I make time to talk through problems and find solutions.

My spouse is very supportive and encourages me to follow my passion.

My spouse and I love to give and serve others.

My spouse and I are an amazing team.

My spouse is my best friend.

I accept my spouse and all their flaws.

I seize the opportunity to apologize first.

I can communicate my feelings and take personal responsibility for my feelings and actions.

I can ask for what I need in my marriage.

I can appreciate that my spouse is ever evolving and continually changing.

I love and support every version of my spouse.

I love, trust, and respect my spouse.

I love my spouse more than the world.

I will remain faithful to my spouse.

I communicate when times are hard in a positive way.

I focus on creating a healthy marriage.

I take responsibility for my emotions.

I avoid blaming and pointing the finger.

I replace anger with understanding and compassion.

I treat my spouse the way I want to be treated.

I choose to respond in love even when it's hard.

I will not disrespect my spouse.

I let go of all grudges and resentment.

I practice patience and give grace to my spouse.

I give my spouse the benefit of the doubt.

I feel safe and secure with my spouse.

I feel loved and cherished by my spouse.

I appreciate everything my spouse does for me.

It feels so good to desire and be desired by my spouse.

We make time for each other.

We understand each other.

We are open with each other.

We are perfect for each other.

Every day our marriage becomes stronger.

Every day our marriage becomes more loving.

I welcome romance into my marriage.

My love for my spouse is unconditional.

My spouse is my greatest blessing.

My spouse and I talk about the things that matter.

My spouse and I work together to resolve conflict.

My spouse comes first, then my family.

My spouse is important to me.

I appreciate and respect how my spouse is different from me.

I see the potential in my spouse.

I support and give my spouse space to become the best version of themselves.

I cannot change my spouse, but I can be the change.

I seek out the right marriage counselors for marriage advice, wisdom, and accountability.

I support my spouse in their decisions.

I support my spouse's goals and dreams.

I respect and take action to fulfill my spouse's needs.

My goal is always to create harmony in my marriage.

I have the best spouse in the world.

I enjoy the safety and security of my marriage.

I experience fun, intimacy, and personal fulfillment in my marriage.

My happiness starts within.

My marriage is a light in this world.

We are an example to our kids and others of a godly marriage.

God is the center of my home and marriage.

God's favor and grace are on my marriage.

My marriage is divinely protected by God.

My marriage is a true gift from God.

DAY 25

Affirmations for Positive Parenting

Your words as a parent have great power.
Use them wisely and make sure they come from the heart.
-Carolina King

At the end of the day, the most overwhelming key
to a child's success is the positive involvement of parents.
-Jane D. Hull

I am a wonderful parent.

I am grateful for my kids and my family.

I am the best mom/dad/caregiver for my child.

I am learning and growing with my child.

I am fair and assertive.

I am prayerful and gracious.

I am the best parent I can be.

I love my child no matter what.

I meet my child where they are.

I pour into and build up my child's self-esteem.

I show my child unconditional love.

I choose to model what I want to see in my child.

I choose to focus on progress, not perfection, for myself and my children.

I don't love the hard times or struggles, but I love my kids.

I love how much joy being a parent gives me.

I deserve all that is good and so do my children.

I can stay calm when my kids are not.

I learn and become a better parent with each passing day.

I give myself permission to set healthy boundaries.

My spouse and I collaborate and agree on positive parenting approaches.

My child and I are a team; we solve problems together.

My child is not giving me a hard time, they are having a hard time, and I can help.

I am a healthy and loving parent.

I am a patient parent.

I am a good listener.

I am my children's comfort and safe place.

I am grateful for and seek out resources to help me parent well.

I am confident and growing in my parenting.

I am using discipline appropriately to help correct my child's behavior.

I intentionally speak to my child in a loving tone.

I can balance my needs with my child's.

I love being a parent.

I teach my children to set boundaries.

I teach my children to be kind and compassionate to others.

I teach my children to love and respect their bodies.

I respond calmly when my child is being disruptive or challenging.

I know taking breaks isn't the same as giving up.

I can't control how I feel, but I can choose to control how I behave.

I make mistakes, and that is ok.

My child makes mistakes and that is okay.

What works for someone else may not work for me or my child.

Parenting has ups and downs, and I can handle them.

When I am wrong, I apologize and say I'm sorry.

Despite the challenges, my children feel loved and safe.

I do what is right and best for me and my children.

I remind my child they are capable of anything they put their mind to.

I will work with a supportive team—family members, friends, teachers, our church community, and even therapists—to help my children succeed.

It's okay to seek out extra help and support when I need it.

I fully support my children in their unique gifts and passions.

I feed my children healthy food options.

I teach my children how to take care of their bodies.

I say "tell me more" often.

I say "I love you" all the time.

I spend plenty of quality time with my children.

I empower and trust my child to solve many problems on their own.

I believe in my child's abilities and skills.

Sometimes my child feels angry or sad, and that's ok.

Pursuing my passions is a great example for my child.

I'm happy that my children openly share their thoughts and feelings with me.

My children don't want perfection; they want me to be there.

My mental and physical health matters as much as my child's.

Being frustrated doesn't make me a bad parent.

It is okay to say no.

When I take care of myself, my kids will also learn to value self-care.

I give myself permission to have an identity outside of being a parent.

I give myself permission to pursue my dreams outside of being a parent.

I'm the best parent for my child.

I'm doing the best I can.

I'm blessed to be a parent.

I learn from my child.

My children do their chores willingly.

My children's health is a priority to me.

My family is free of disease and illness.

Good health is a priority for me and my family.

I get rest when I need it.

I take care of my mental and emotional health for myself and for my family.

We stay fit and love to exercise.

Having meals together is enjoyable for our family.

We are making great memories for our children.

We have lots of fun in our home.

All of my children feel safe and cared for by me.

My child has a great future ahead.

Comparisons do not serve me as a parent.

Our home is a place of peace.

Our home is full of love.

Today is a new day for me as a parent.

Life is good in my family.

I teach and train my children how to make good and godly decisions.

I raise strong, confident children.

I raise children who love God and love others.

DAY 26

Affirmations for Healing a Broken Heart

To be rejected by someone doesn't mean you should also reject yourself or that you should think of yourself as a lesser person.
-Jocelyn Soriano

Every time I thought I was being rejected from something good, I was actually being re-directed to something better.
-Steve Maraboli

I am valuable and worthy.

I am able to heal.

I am lovable.

I am okay.

I am letting go of what doesn't serve me.

I am open to the possibility that this relationship was not in my best interest.

I am on my way to something even better.

I am free to be the best version of me

I am free to begin again.

I release my past.

I release these chains.

I release myself from all regrets and disappointments.

I matter, no matter how I feel.

I know my worth, even if someone else doesn't.

I choose to have the strength to move on.

I choose to let go of this anger.

I choose happiness today instead of dwelling on my past dissappointments.

I love and accept myself no matter what.

I love myself unconditionally.

This pain is temporary.

This pain will lessen.

I will get through this.

I will heal from this.

I will love again.

I will find joy in life again.

I will love myself the way I deserve to be loved.

I will take time away for personal and spiritual growth.

There is no relationship loss that I cannot overcome.

I do not deserve abuse.

Healing begins within me.

I forgive myself.

I forgive myself unconditionally.

I forgive myself for all the mistakes I've made.

I forgive the person that hurt me.

My heart will heal, and I will have peace.

My breakup is an opportunity for me to be free and live my best life.

It's time to let go of them and let go of bitterness.

I stand firm on my principles and values.

I have a lot to offer, and I am enough.

I have faith that there is a divine plan for my love life.

I am open to only healthy and positive relationships.

I am blessed because I am moving on.

I am excited about this new beginning.

I am capable of loving again.

I am more than this breakup.

I am strong enough to heal from this broken heart.

I trust that this ending is for my highest good.

It's perfectly normal to feel this way after a breakup.

I am grateful for the lessons.

I am completely whole and perfect by myself.

I am deserving of love.

I am complete on my own.

I am healing more and more every day.

I am working on me, for me.

My life is full of blessings. I look forward to tomorrow.

I trust that everything will work out for my good.

It is getting easier day by day.

There is someone amazing waiting for me.

No matter what happens in my life, I still love myself.

I find strength in God.

The best is yet to come.

DAY 27

Affirmations for Letting Go and Moving Forward

Pain will leave you, when you let go.
-Jeremy Aldana

Accept yourself, love yourself, and keep moving forward.
If you want to fly, you have to give up what weighs you down.
-Rov T. Bennett

I am free.

I am free from worry.

I am free of the pain.

I am free of burdens.

I am free from my past mistakes.

I am free to be me.

I let go.

I let go of pain.

I let go of anger.

I let go of regrets.

I let go of fear.

I let go of past relationships that are not right for me.

I release the grudges I held in the past, and I am free.

I release all the baggage that has stopped me from moving forward.

I release the burden of shame, guilt, and self-judgment.

I release all stress and criticisms.

I forgive myself and let go of all the feelings and mindsets that hold me back.

I forgive those who have harmed me in the past and peacefully detach from them.

I forgive those who wronged me.

I choose not to be around people who make me feel worthless or unhappy.

I don't need toxic people in my life.

I love and accept my family members exactly as they are.

I unconditionally love my family even if they do not understand me completely.

I am healing at my own pace, and I will be at peace.

I am healed and whole.

I am not afraid to move on.

I am accepting of my imperfections.

I am capable of loving all of who I am.

I am not my past.

I am letting go of the past.

I am over it.

I am so much more than my past mistakes.

I am empowered to live free when I let go.

I am ready to let go and move on with my life.

I am leaving the past behind and pressing forward.

I am letting go of everything that stresses me out.

I am focusing on the positive and shifting towards a happier mindset.

I let go of resentment and any other feeling that doesn't positively help me.

I let go of the need to control others.

I let go of all unrealistic expectations.

I let go of all urges to criticize myself.

I can face challenges and stand back up after a setback.

I can overcome everything that comes my way.

My spirit is renewed and free.

My past does not define me.

My mind is free from distractions.

My strength is greater than any struggle.

I embrace this new season of my life.

I live my life without restraints.

I allow myself to be forgiven.

I choose to take time for myself.

I have struggled enough, and it ends today.

I will stop worrying and find a solution.

I stop holding things against others.

I say goodbye to all the negativity.

I say goodbye to things that block my mental and spiritual growth.

I will not let the pain of the past keep me from moving forward.

I free myself from fear of the unknown.

I overcome self-condemnation and choose to love myself unconditionally.

I let go of everything that worries me.

I choose freedom and release all things that block my blessings.

I have learned all the lessons, and I'm ready to let go.

I have the power to let go of my past and move on.

I move beyond my mistakes.

I focus solely on what I can control and let go of what I cannot.

I leave behind the old me and embrace the new me.

I'm open to a better future.

I choose to thrive and enjoy my life.

I hold on to the positive memories and let go of negative ones.

Letting go of my pain helps me heal.

I am not my past. I let go and let God.

I am worthy of God's best for my life.

Affirmations to Level Up Your Productivity

DAY 28

Affirmations to Develop a Success Mindset

To change your life, you have to change yourself.
To change yourself, you have to change your mindset.
-Wilson Kanadi

Your life is as good as your mindset.
-Unknown

I am worthy of success.

I am intelligent, insightful, and wise.

I am skillful, talented, and gifted.

I am strong, brave, and confident.

I am capable of achieving greatness.

I am open to limitless possibilities.

I choose to embrace the best version of myself.

I choose faith over fear.

I say yes to new opportunities.

I envision a prosperous future for myself.

I don't just seek opportunities, I create them.

I have everything I need to be successful.

I turn failures into stepping stones and setbacks into comebacks.

I was born to do great things.

I don't need anyone's permission to be successful.

My great work ethic will be rewarded.

My thoughts are free of self-imposed limitations.

My mind is laser-focused on hitting my daily, weekly and monthly goals.

My income is always increasing.

My financial future is full and fruitful.

I achieve whatever I set my mind to.

I pursue my goals relentlessly until they are obtained.

I believe in my ability to be successful.

I have the power to transform my life.

I overcome all obstacles and challenges that stand between me and success.

I have the right mentors to help me achieve my success aspirations.

I am smart. All my ideas bring profit.

I am my best source of motivation.

I see opportunities everywhere.

I am developing a detailed plan to achieve my goals.

I am willing to do whatever it takes to increase my income and succeed.

I am proud of myself and all that I have accomplished.

I am open to becoming a successful entrepreneur.

I am more than my mistakes.

I am at peace with who I am.

I am creating a life I love.

I am relentless in the pursuit of success.

I am highly motivated and productive.

I take charge of my financial situation.

I spend less than I earn.

I give myself permission to prosper.

I release all negative thoughts and mindsets about wealth and prosperity.

I have the ability to reach all my personal and financial goals.

I welcome success in all areas of my life.

I find it easy to believe in myself.

I have a positive attitude, and I never quit.

I celebrate my own success and the success of others.

I will leave a legacy for my family.

Working smarter, not harder, comes naturally to me.

My progress is getting me closer to where I want to be.

Every day, in every way, I am becoming a better version of myself.

Being successful is my birthright.

DAY 29

Affirmations to Help You Achieve Your Goals

We all have big dreams, high hopes, and grand plans. You are chosen to do great, big, world-changing, culture-shattering, life-giving, audacious things. The problem is most of us get tricked out of starting small. The truth is– the bigger the dream, sometimes, the smaller the start.
-Ruth Jones

A dream written down with a date becomes a goal.
A goal broken down into steps becomes a plan.
A plan backed by action makes your dreams come true.
-Greg Reid

I am capable of achieving great things.

I am worthy of all my biggest goals and dreams.

I am totally committed to making my goals a reality.

I can. I will. I must.

I can achieve anything I want.

I can do hard things.

I can do this, because I've got this.

I can accomplish anything I focus on.

Everything that I want is within my reach.

Everything I do turns into success.

I have what it takes to reach my goals.

I have what it takes to succeed and thrive.

I have what it takes to be successful in all that I do.

I have an abundance of opportunities to achieve my goals and dreams.

My success is now, and I am unstoppable.

Anything is possible for my life.

I am highly productive.

I am capable, consistent, and strong.

I am optimistic about my future.

I am focused and intentionally working towards my goals daily.

Achieving my goals allows me to live my best life.

I surpass all my goals with ease.

I am focused on completing all my action steps.

I step out of my comfort zone to achieve my goals.

I believe in myself and my abilities.

I release limits and boundaries.

I achieve more success than I can possibly imagine.

I take huge steps towards my goals each day.

I surround myself with people who encourage me to reach my goals.

I exercise discipline, patience, and perseverance.

I am daily growing into the person I need to be to achieve my goals.

Day after day I step closer to achieving my goals.

As long as I take action, I can achieve my goals.

What I am seeking is seeking me.

DAY 30

Affirmations to Stay Focused

I don't care how much power, brilliance or energy you have,
if you don't harness it and focus it on a specific target,
and hold it there you're never going to accomplish
as much as your ability warrants.
-Zig Ziglar

Where focus goes, energy flows.
And if you don't take the time to focus on what matters,
then you're living a life of someone else's design.
-Tony Robbins

I am focused on the task at hand.

I am present.

I am not distracted.

I am an expert at time management.

I am alert and attentive at all times.

I am free of confusion.

My mind is clear and focused.

My concentration grows stronger every day.

My attention is undivided.

By focusing on the best things in my life, I give them power to grow and multiply.

Focusing on the present moment improves my concentration and productivity.

Giving each moment my undivided attention, creates endless inspiration for me.

Because I am focused on what I am doing, I get the results I desire.

I easily concentrate on every task I perform.

I easily get into the flow whenever required.

I release scattered thoughts and return my focus to the present moment.

I ignore everything that attempts to disturb my concentration and momentum.

I focus my mind easily and quickly.

I focus my attention on my top priorities in life.

I focus my mind only on those things which are aligned with my goals.

I focus my thoughts on what I want, and I take action towards that purpose.

I focus my priorities on success and prosperity.

My concentrated efforts are paying off.

My focus is a key to my success.

Right now, I focus only on this priority.

Nothing distracts me.

Being focused comes easily to me.

As long as I keep my thoughts on my goals, I easily maintain my focus and momentum.

Because my life is clutter-free, my mind is clear, attentive, and focused.

Being in the zone is something I strive to attain and maintain every day.

I am fully focused and present in all interactions with others.

I am focused on realizing all of my dreams.

I keep my thoughts on my goals.

I free myself from distractions.

I have a singular focus.

I give myself permission to turn off whatever is distracting me.

I have clarity and energy.

I center my thoughts on what I am doing.

I will accomplish everything I need to do today.

I commit myself to developing the highest level of focus in my life.

I do one task at a time.

I seek improvement, not perfection.

I can focus my attention at will.

I can do what needs to be done.

I focus on each activity throughout my day.

I focus on the end result.

I focus on excellence in all that I do.

I am focused and in my zone.

DAY 31

Affirmations to Overcome Procrastination

Sometimes the smallest step in the right direction ends up being the biggest step of your life. Tiptoe if you must, but take a step.
-Naeem Callaway

Procrastination is the enemy of success.
-Unknown

I am a doer.

I am proactive.

I am disciplined.

I am grounded, focused, and attentive.

I am competent, committed, and diligent.

I am positive, proactive, and productive.

I am motivated to finish my tasks.

I do what needs doing even if it is hard or boring.

Fear cannot stop me.

Nothing will stand in my way of accomplishing my tasks and making progress.

I accept no excuses, just results.

The best time to start something new is right now.

All of my problems have solutions.

Although I make mistakes, I never quit.

Today, I abandon my old habits and take up new, more positive ones.

Today, I will take positive action towards my goals.

Today, I stop letting things distract me from reaching my goals.

Today, no matter what, I will focus on my number one priority.

Every small step I take makes a big difference.

Every day I am moving my life forward.

Every act of discipline creates more freedom for my future.

Everything I do today leads me to a better tomorrow.

I believe in myself and my abilities.

I believe my hard work is paying off.

By finishing my tasks now, I give my future self the gift of freedom.

By taking care of this present moment, I set myself up for a beautiful future.

I can do hard things.

I can do anything I set my mind to.

I can focus and concentrate at will.

I can accomplish everything that needs to get completed today.

I may make mistakes, but I don't quit.

I concentrate all my efforts on the things I want to accomplish in life.

I've got this.

I may stumble, but I never stay down.

I give myself permission to be imperfect.

I release negativity; Instead, I focus on positivity, productivity, and progress.

I release negative thoughts and choose to approach each task with confidence and positivity.

I choose to just get started rather than wait on perfect conditions.

I maximize the time I have.

I execute on the plans I've created.

I get things done fast.

I never put things off.

I tackle hard things first.

I work hard even though I may feel tired.

I work hard even when I don't feel like working.

My work ethic is stronger than my feelings.

My ability to conquer my challenges is limitless.

My potential to succeed is infinite.

My future self will thank me for all that I'm doing right now.

I love taking action.

I love taking action to accomplish my goals.

I am in control of my thoughts, choices, and actions.

I am committed to being focused on my goals because I am worth it.

I am equipped with all the tools I need to complete the task in front of me.

I am determined to get everything done.

I am not afraid to try and fail. I welcome the growth that comes from these experiences.

I am able to release negative thoughts and feelings that do not serve me.

I have the ability to focus on what needs to get done.

I have the willpower to complete my assignments.

I have clarity and energy.

I make time to do what's on my to do list.

I allow myself to focus on one small step at a time.

I will complete my number one priority today.

I will make good use of my time.

I take care of the future by taking care of the present.

I take one step at a time and get closer to completing my tasks.

I approach my tasks with confidence and enthusiasm.

I free myself from the paralysis of perfection.

I act quickly.

I hate wasting my time. I take immediate action.

I break all my goals into small, manageable steps.

I'm stronger than my procrastination.

I'm not afraid of doing hard things.

I'm excited to get this done and celebrate the results.

I'm getting closer to my dream life one day at a time.

ABOUT THE AUTHOR

Lou Jones is a speaker, life coach, and minister of the gospel who has motivated audiences of all ages with powerful keynotes, workshops, and coaching sessions that have helped thousands transform their lives. Pulling from his own personal trials and triumphs, Lou inspires and equips people to live their lives to the fullest and maximize their potential. He lives in Dallas, Texas, with his wife, Ruth, and their son Aiden.

- @loujonesinspires
- @loujonesinspires
- @loujonesinspires
- @loujonesinspires
- @loujonesinspires
- @loujonesinspire
- loujones.com

ACKNOWLEDGEMENTS

I'm deeply grateful to you, God, for the inspiration to write this book. For over a year, I sought your guidance, fervently listening for your direction and the specific book I was meant to write. When I was sensitive enough to hear you, your response surprised me—not just one book, but multiple. I am eternally at your service, and my heart overflows with gratitude.

To begin this journey of gratitude, I want to acknowledge the incredible strength embodied in a woman I hold dear—my mother, Gloria Jones. You've transcended the role of a parent; you've been my friend, mentor, wise counselor, supporter, and encourager. The unstoppable man I am today owes its existence to you.

To my remarkable wife, Ruth, you stand as a testament to God's faithfulness in my life. What I believed for, you've exceeded beyond my wildest expectations. You are my inspiration, confidant, biggest cheerleader, partner, and strategist. As the first author in our family, you've paved the way, contributing as my editor, designer, and publisher. Because of your sacrifice, this book has been published, as testimony to the collaborative strength that defines our life together. You are the greatest wife and friend a man could ask for. Thank you for being such a wonderful mother to our son, Aiden, and for being the glue that holds our beautiful family together.

Aiden, my lion-like leader—my son—you bring immeasurable blessing to my life. I can't imagine life without you, and I'm honored to be your father. Thank you for your unconditional love.

A heartfelt shout-out to my Detroit circle of friends—Ajay, Carl and April, Vern and Erica, Sheronda, Kim, Deidre, Monique, and many others. I remember when you all blessed me with a silver bracelet engraved with "Pastor Lou" on the front and "Entrusted to Lead" on the back. Your support and encouragement still resonate in my spirit.

To my Phoenix friends, especially my Phoenix mother June, thank you for your love and support. Quintin, your friendship and support has been a true blessing in my life. Thank you for helping me step into my entrepreneurial gift.

The roots of my connection to affirmations trace back to my beloved high school history teacher, Mr. Robert Lichtman. Thank you for introducing me to the unstoppable influence of affirmations, fostering not only my leadership skills but also my passion for education.

To the numerous friends and family who've shaped my life's path, your kind words, belief in me, and unwavering support are etched in my heart and prayers.

Finally, to everyone who has been part of my journey, whether online followers or those I've met in person, my God-given mission is you. I aim to inspire and equip you to reach your fullest potential. May this book be a catalyst, helping you level up in life and become unstoppable.

REFERENCES

Cooke, R., Trebaczyk, H., Harris, P., & Wright, A.J. (2014) Self-affirmation promotes physical activity. Journal of Sport and Exercise Psychology, 36(2), 217–223.

Critcher, C. R., & Dunning, D. (2015). Self-affirmations provide a broader perspective on self-threat. Personality and Social Psychology Bulletin, 41(1), 3-18.

Epton, T., & Harris, P.R. (2008). Self-affirmation promotes health behavior change. Health Psychology, 27(6), 746-752.

Gu, R., Yang, J., Yang, Z. et al. Self-affirmation enhances the processing of uncertainty: An event-related potential study. Cogn Affect Behav Neurosci 19, 327–337 (2019). https://doi.org/10.3758/s13415-018-00673-0

Harris, P. R., Mayle, K., Mabbott, L., & Napper, L. (2007). Self-affirmation reduces smokers' defensiveness to graphic on-pack cigarette warning labels. Health Psychology, 26, 437–446.

Koole, S.L., Smeets, K., van Knippenberg, A., Dijksterhuis, A. (1999). The cessation of rumination through self-affirmation. Journal of Personality and Social Psychology, 77, 111–125.

Layous, K., Davis, E. M., Garcia, J., Purdie-Vaughns, V., Cook, J. E., & Cohen, G. L. (2017). Feeling left out, but affirmed: Protecting against the negative effects of low belonging in college. Journal of Experimental Social Psychology, 69, 227-231.

Logel, C., & Cohen, G.L. (2012). The role of the self in physical health: Testing the effect of a values-affirmation intervention on weight loss. Psychological Science, 23(1), 53–55.

Sherman, D. K., Cohen, G. L., Nelson, L. D., Nussbaum, A. D., Bunyan, D. P., & Garcia, J. (2009). Affirmed yet unaware: Exploring the role of awareness in the process of self-affirmation. Journal of Personality and Social Psychology, 97, 745-764.

Wiesenfeld, B.M., Brockner, J., Petzall, B., Wolf, R., & Bailey J. (2001). Stress and coping among layoff survivors: A self-affirmation analysis. Anxiety, Stress and Coping: An International Journal, 14, 15–34.

TRANSFORM YOUR LIFE, MINDSET, AND SPIRIT

with the Unstoppable
Motivation on Demand Bundle

Get your bundle now:
loujones.com/unstoppable

Unlock boundless motivation with our tools designed to help you feel inspired and empowered, gain confidence, and walk in victory and peace.

Your journey to unstoppable motivation
STARTS HERE!

www.ingramcontent.com/pod-product-compliance
Lightning Source LLC
LaVergne TN
LVHW021715060526
838200LV00050B/2678